MIDLANDS CANALS

MEMORIES OF THE CANAL CARRIERS

Birthday present from Rhian & Brian
65TH received 20/07/2007

MIDLANDS CANALS

MEMORIES OF THE CANAL CARRIERS

ROBERT DAVIES

First published in 2006 by Tempus Publishing
Reprinted 2007

Reprinted in 2009 by
The History Press
The Mill, Brimscombe Port,
Stroud, Gloucestershire, GL5 2QG
www.thehistorypress.co.uk

British Library Cataloguing in Publication Data.
A catalogue record for this book is available from the British Library.

ISBN 978 0 7524 3910 5

Typesetting and origination by
Tempus Publishing Limited.
Printed in Great Britain.

Contents

People, Time and Photographs

The Bible's well-used formula 'three score years and ten' for a generation still seems applicable in what we refer to as the 'modern age'. But it is a specific generation that we now focus our attention on, for the men and women that were born in the 1930s and 1940s are the subject of this book. Their mode of living and working on the inland waterways of Britain has, in recent years, become of great interest, because it was a way of life that has simply disappeared. It is as thoroughly lost as that of the ancient Egyptians. Fortunately, over the last five years or so it has been my privilege to interview a small group of these boat men and women, the survivors of that period, to hear their stories. It must be said that as a generation they are disappearing fast. Now a new generation are taking to the canals in a type of recreational craft that would have been thought impossible only fifty years ago. Disenchanted with this computer age and its amazing and multitudinous technologies, they may have acquired a rather rose-tinted impression of what it was actually like to work for a canal carrying company, a view that these pages will probably dispel. For who really wants to start work at 4 or 5 a.m. by collecting a horse from a stable, shovel tons of coal from a boat's hold in the rain, and then carry on working until it is too dark to see?

And what about the changes for women? Some may complain that there are still inequalities, but back in 1950, women working as long a day as their men folk were paid nothing. The father or husband of the family received the pay-packet and it was up to him as to how it would be distributed. This may sound harsh from our modern perspective, but as far as employers were concerned in those not too distant times, wives and daughters were treated no better than one of the company's horses; they were fed and watered and worked just as long hours.

To do the interviews justice, I had to search for decent photographs to illustrate both the living and working conditions of the period. Luckily, some of my subjects had a handful of photographs to call on, though many of those were in a bad condition. Unfortunately there were few cameras about in those days, and few working people could afford one or wanted one. But there is another fact to take into account. Most boat people consider their life to have been totally mundane, and still to this day find it hard to understand why anyone in their right mind would be interested in their unglamorous daily activities.

Do you remember the 1960s? Then you must be getting along in years; yet, ironically, many youngsters of today also connect with that tumultuous decade because some of the fashions and music of that period have gone through a revival. Perhaps that decade was one of the strangest transitional periods in history, as Britain and Europe recovered from the ravages of the Second World War. Britian's economy and therefore its forms of transport began to prosper, with the advantage of passing some of that wealth to the youth.

For me, the 1960s meant The Beatles and the Rolling Stones, the miniskirt and flower power. Neil Armstrong was walking on the moon in 1969 but, strangely enough, 'Caggy' Stevens was still walking his horse around the BCN. Even in the 'high-tech' decade of the 1960s, Britain's waterways were still providing a valuable corridor for goods and raw materials.

Fortunately there were a few photographers about to capture boating activity, which brings me to a friend of mine, David Wilson. It is always exciting to unearth hitherto unseen photographs from canal history, especially when they convey so much information about the canal-carrying past. Usually, though, these images are often victims of neglect, full of blemishes, scratches and missing corners. Not so with David's images, for he travelled throughout England during the 1960s and early 1970s using a range of personal conveyance with a keen desire to capture all types of transport. Like many transport enthusiasts, David had, and still has, a love for steam railways and canals. Steam was his first love, but canals came a close second, and his evocative high-quality black and white photographs add more to our knowledge of those days. So I shall kick off with some of David's pictures before embarking on the interviews. I can only apologise for the first section of photographs and indeed a goodly proportion of the interviews tending to hover around the BCN, but you will soon discover that other boat men and women worked the northern and southern canals.

The first three shots are of Thomas Clayton's oil boats, operating in the West Bromwich area. They are all on short-haul voyages from local gas works along to Oldbury Tar Works. The first image is extremely interesting because it shows a technique that I have never before seen photographed; that of stemming up. This is essentially where the motor boat is used to push the boat in front. It was a method utilised when there was no one else to steer the second boat if it was towed. I spoke to Enoch Clowes who worked for Claytons about this unusual operation, because I imagined the procedure would be so difficult as to make it almost impossible. Enoch assured me that 'stemmin em', as he referred to it, was really quite simple after a bit of practice, and that even tight bends in the canal could be negotiated smoothly once your brain had learned the trick of concentrating on the actions of the boat in front.

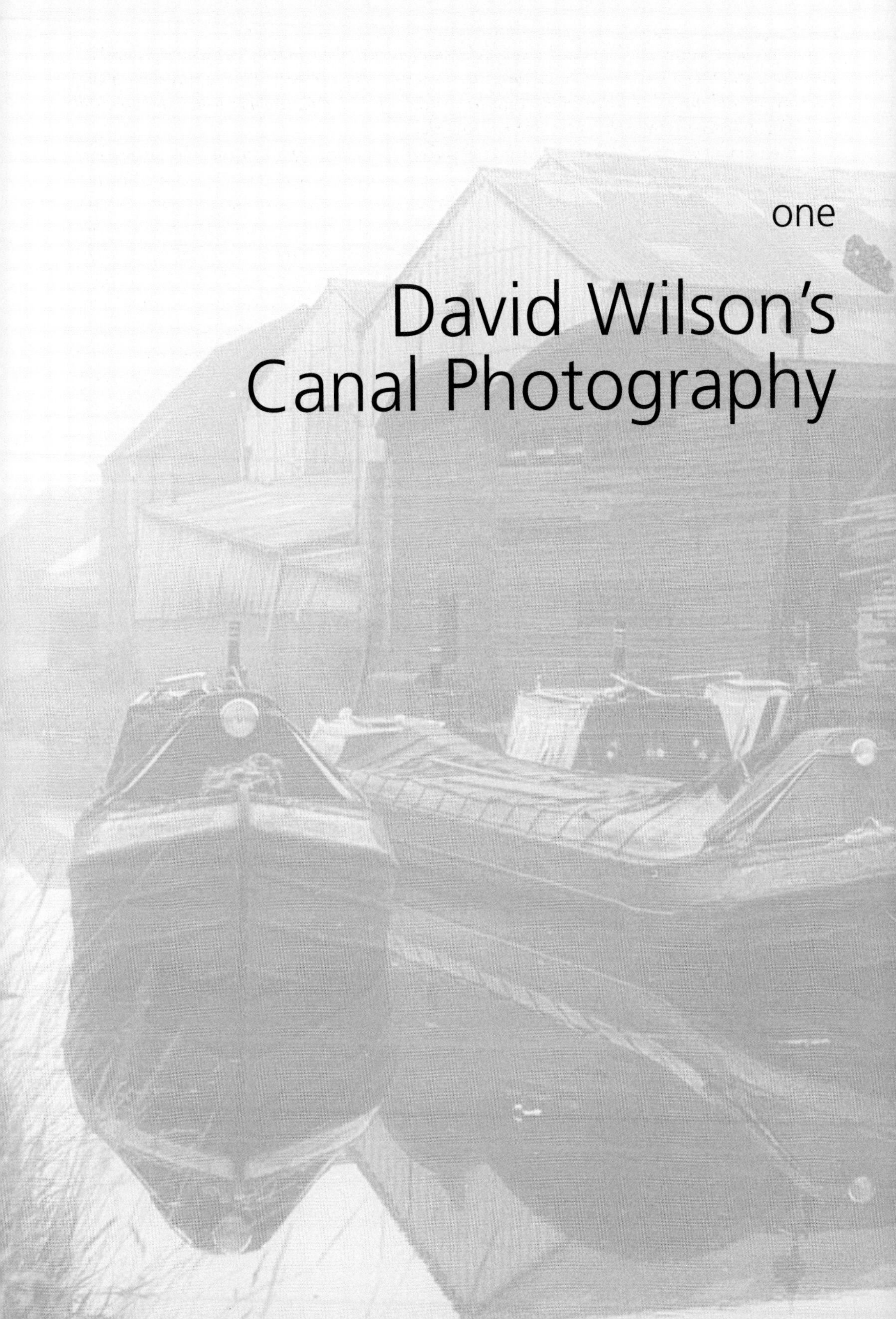

one

David Wilson's Canal Photography

THOS CLAYTON
TOWY
No 9

Above: James Monk's boat *Irwell* at Patricroft heading toward the Barton Aqueduct. The *Irwell* was built in 1934 for Canal Transport Ltd. (D.W.)

Marster's coal wharf and yard at Ocker Hill is interesting for two reasons: firstly, because in recent years it has become the site of the Midland headquarters of British Waterways, and demonstrates how drastically the character and function of a place changes as the years go by. The short arm is now frequented by pleasure craft, but in the past it was an important extraction point for water for the Birmingham Canal Navigation's depot some way up the hill; secondly, because it shows the layout and activities of a coal yard. The photograph includes a motor boat with three day boats, the one in the distance being emptied out by one man plus a shovel. Much of the work in the coal trade was performed by laborious dirty hand toil, with simple implements like the coal barrows in the distance. Marster's coal yard was typical of hundreds like it in the Midlands and elsewhere, when the country depended on its coal production and distribution for its industrial and domestic power and heat.

Opposite above: Bill Beech steers one of Thomas Clayton's oil boats, while demonstrating the art of stemming as he pushes the loaded butty boat on the short stretch from Swan Village Gas Works at West Bromwich to the Oldbury Tar Works on the Old Main Line.

Opposite middle: Thomas Clayton's *Towy* is seen halfway up the Ryder's Green flight of locks at Great Bridge, Tipton, on 22 June 1965. The captain is probably Freddy King and he is carrying liquid by-products from Walsall Gas Works to Oldbury Tar Works. (D.W.)

Opposite below: Thomas Clayton's motor boat *Tay* sports a simpler sign writing as it leaves the Walsall Canal and enters the BCN Main Line Canal at Pudding Green Junction. (D.W.)

Above: A typical BCN tug and a three-day or Joey boat at Marster's coal wharf, Tipton, on 13 August 1966. Notice how the coal is piled into three rucks in each boat. (D.W.)

Below: Braunston, the busy junction of the Oxford and Grand Union Canal in Northamptonshire, 24 October 1965. In the distance is the toll house, now information centre, and behind that a fine example of a Horseley Bridge. The pair of empty boats in the foreground are probably British Waterways, and definitely ex-Grand Union. (D.W.)

Right: 26 September 1966. Tailby & Cox's wood yard, Great Bridge, Tipton. These are all ex-Grand Union boats, now being worked by Willow Wren. This particular arm, the Haines branch, came into Great Bridge from a junction on the Walsall Canal just below Ryder's Green locks. The boats have all been reversed onto this short arm. The boat on the far right is the *Renfrew* and the one on the left is possibly *Hawksbury*. The *Renfrew* previously belonged to Lady Line. In the picture are three motors and one butty.

Middle: A pair of wide boats working the Bridgewater Canal not far from the Barton Aqueduct, 6 October 1970. (D.W.)

Below: D&R Houlston Canal Carriers motor boat *Parrot* based on the Staffordshire & Worcestershire Canal at Kinver. (D.W.)

WILLOW WREN C. T. S. LTD
HAYES RD
SOUTHALL
MIDDX
HAYES 2277-8
BRENTFORD
CYGNUS

October 1965. A pair of Willow Wren boats, motor and butty, *Redshank* and *Greenshank*, leaving Braunston behind. They are both ex-Grand Union boats, and were called *Reading* and *Bawtry* prior to their sale.

The dog on the butty is obviously keeping an eye on progress, while the young man in the hatches is decidedly relaxed with the tiller resting on his shoulder. These are some of the earliest boats that Willow Wren purchased. Companies like Willow Wren, Claytons, and Birmingham & Midland Canal Carriers were managing small fleets of boats, and there were still the one-man bands like Robert Tudor Coal Carriers, who were typical of dozens of small coal traders that had operated during the first half of the twentieth century. Tudor had a coal wharf just off Pudding Green Junction. In the late 1950s he had just two open-day boats, both drawn by horse, but in the following decade he operated a motor boat and lorry. His coal came from the Sandwell colliery, less than two miles away on the Old Main Line. After delivery at his wharf, the coal was weighed, bagged, and sent on to his customers by road.

Opposite above: A close-up view of the Willow Wren pair *Coleshill* and *Cygnus* at Great Bridge shows a young lad in the hatches. (D.W.)

Opposite below: A Robert Tudor Coal Carrier boat at Pudding Green Junction, Birmingham–Wolverhampton Main Line Canal/Walsall Canal, 21 June 1965. Tudor used to operate from Albion Wharf, just under the Albion Bridge, which is the concrete bridge in the background. (D.W.)

A pair of Willow Wren boats lie at Tailby & Cox's timber yard at Great Bridge after unloading on 8 June 1966. The pair – *Coleshill* and *Cygnus* – are though to have been captained by Ray White along with his wife. (D.W.)

A boat belonging to the Anderton Carrying Co., near Spon Lane Bridge, West Bromwich, in the late 1960s. (D.W.)

two

Potbanks and Knobsticks

Jim and Joyce Moore, 2000.

Jim and Joyce Moore talk about their life on the Trent & Mersey Canal.

Joyce

I was born on a narrow boat in 1934, not far from the Anderton lift. My parents had earlier worked for Potter & Sons of Runcorn, but were now working for the Anderton Canal Carrying Co. This particular company had a long history going back to 1836, before which time it traded as Alexander Reid & Co. Toward the end of the nineteenth, and early twentieth century, it was run by the family of Boddington, until it was bought by the Mersey Weavers in 1954. The Anderton Co. and its boats were popularly known as Knobsticks, and though there is uncertainty over where this unusual name originated, it may have arisen from the stick that the company marshall carried during his horse-back rides around the canal system as he checked on the boats' activities.

Opposite above: Joyce working Red Bull Lock with the British Waterways boat *Birdswood*.

Opposite below: Jim at Manchester Docks with British Waterways boats *Minnow* and *Alsager*, in the late 1950s.

Opposite: The cabin of *Birdswood* near Kidsgrove on the Trent & Mersey Canal in the early 1960s. Notice the antique radio next to the chimney. The decorative art work looks like traditional sign-writing but is, in fact, transfers.

Right: Jim is unloading bentonite clay at Longport Wharf out of the hold of *Birdswood*, *c.*1960.

Below: The Mersey Weavers boat *William* is loaded with flour and destined for the Silverdale Coop at Etruria, 1952.

Another family that worked for Knobsticks was Albert and Florry Atkins. They were good friends of my parents, and when I was thirteen, Florry approached me, and asked if I would like to go and work on their boat, helping out with their two children, and doing other boat chores. I decided to go with them, and we got on really well. In fact many of the boat people at this time were like an extended family, where everyone knew everyone else's business, but in the kindest way.

The Atkins children were then aged ten and six, and I learned to wash, cook, keep the boat clean, and play games with them such as dominoes. At night I would put them to bed. It amazes me even today, now that I live in a house, how we managed to cook so much in that small space, on those tiny ranges. I did more baking in those days than ever I have when living on the bank.

The Atkins paid me five shillings for every trip we made, and much of our carrying dealt with the transporting of crates from the Potteries up to Weston Point on the Mersey. The crates were full of finished products from the pottery works that included plates, cups and saucers and a multitude of dishes; many of them for export. All the pieces were carefully packed inside crates using straw to prevent breakage during transport, many of which were made of wood, and barrel shaped. They were craned on and off the boats. We also carried the raw materials to the Potbanks, just like Jim and many others. I left the Atkins family when I was sixteen and spent a few months with British Waterways before marrying Jim. We married in October 1951 and immediately went to work for the Mersey Weavers, as we referred to the company.

Jim

My mother and father were Jim and Liza Moore. They had worked for Fellows Morton & Clayton in the past, but moved to the Anderton Co. when I was born in 1929. Their boat was the *Pansy*, and based at Burslem. We carried raw materials for the pottery companies in Stoke-on-Trent. These materials included china clay from Cornwall, bentonite, and flint. They were loaded from the large stock piles at Weston Point docks, and carried 'uphill' to a variety of pottery companies – the Potbanks, situated along the Trent & Mersey at Stoke-on-Trent. The trip to and from Weston Point included the use of the Anderton lift, which lowered us down on to the river Weaver. On occasions we used the lift two or three times a day.

When using the Anderton lift, we were given a ticket at Weston Point, which was thirteen miles along the Weaver from the lift. On arriving at the lift, you would take your boat into the large tank, possibly with a second boat. The gate behind you would be closed, and up you went. When at the top, the forward gates opened hydraulically, and out you came. The whole process took some ten to fifteen minutes, just long enough to brew a cup of tea.

Then as you headed for the Harecastle tunnel, you collected a second ticket from Dock Bridge. The tunnel was one-way working, and the directions changed regularly throughout the day, with the last possible traffic at 10 p.m. to Kidsgrove.

My father, who was a bit of a nomad like many boat people, often changed companies, which included Potters, Rayners, FMC and Thomas Clayton's of Oldbury. However, we only did three trips for that last firm, because my dad quickly came to the conclusion that the horse he was given was no good. Apparently this particular horse liked to stop at regular intervals, and once he had taken it into his head to rest it was impossible to get him going again. So after many frustrated efforts and heated words it was back to FMC at Saltley near Birmingham. The motor boat we had there was called *The Count*.

Joyce

After getting married we went boating for Mersey Weavers, who carried from Longport (Stoke) Tunstall and Burslem. Mersey Weavers were a smaller company than Andertons, though between the wars it had operated a peak of around seventy boats. When Jim and I worked for them, in the 1950s I guess that that number had reduced to about thirty. Wages at that time was £4 10*s* for a trip (£4.50), and you got an extra pound if you boated over 400 miles. Many of those trips were in to Manchester, where we delivered gravel that had been loaded at Burslem (Stoke) then we would load up with flour from one of the many Manchester mills and bring it back perhaps to Longport or Stoke. Flour was packed in sacks that were then measured in the old units known as hundred weights (or cwt for short).

Side and top cloths were necessary for keeping the goods dry. Many deliveries of flour were made near Stoke for the Coop in Burslem.

Mersey Weavers had been run for years by the Shirley family, originally a Mr C.W. Shirley, but in our time it had come down to the son, Leslie Shirley. He was then the big boss of the day, but most employees used to think that he was completely crackers. Mr Shirley had a particular affection for whiskey, and on occasions at the yard after a dram or two, he would throw a tantrum and sack everyone that he could see. Of course we all got used to this eccentric behaviour and no one took any real notice, we simply got on with our work. However the real brains behind the carrying operations was a Mr Massey, and he was a true gentleman and always under full control. He worked in the office at Longport, which was more like a double house having two bay windows. This office was situated only yards from the canal. Opposite the office was a long warehouse come shed where salt was packed by six women who were employed for this boring and laborious task.

Jim

Our boat after getting married was the *William* and we later towed a butty with it. Both boats were of wood construction, 72 ft long, and William was powered by a 9hp Bollinder. To appreciate those times it's necessary to understand that in the early 1950s, many items were still rationed from the last war, and we had few possessions that we could call our own. Joyce and I still laugh at the fact that we could only afford one striped towel for bathing, and we had to dry that over the brass rail in the cabin before the second person could use it.

Joyce

Washing ourselves and our clothes all took place in a tin bath, and we regularly took our clean water from the stand pipes that were dotted around the system for that purpose. We never took water out of the canal for washing as some people erroneously think. During the 1950s we carried all the kinds of raw materials, such as bentonite clay that had been brought to the potteries since the time of Josiah Wedgwood in the 1770s. Thousands of tons of clay came by boat from Italy, along with soda ash, flint, salt and other materials all used in the manufacture of pottery.

The boats belonging to Mersey Weavers were decorated with grained surfaces inside, while outside they had black panels with white lettering. At Weston Point, boats were loaded from tubs or sometimes barrows, and the stone or clay, was arranged into two piles in each boat. There were around eight to nine tons in the front pile or 'ruck', and eleven in the rear pile, just in front of the cabin, totalling some 20 tons. The butty was loaded in the same way.

We left Mersey Weavers in 1954, the year that they took over the Anderton Co., and we went boating for Gordon Waddington, who carried coal from Leigh to Runcorn. Waddington's was only a small firm with about half a dozen boats, and we only stayed with them for a short time because their boats were in poor condition and leaked like a sieve. If you left them for any length of time you were always worried that they would sink before you came back. During one winter, the iron butty hit thick ice which ripped a hole in its side. Jim and I had to act quickly to rescue the pups that our pet Collie had just given birth to. The poor cold things had to learn to swim at a very early age. Our final work on the Trent & Mersey was for the nationalised British Waterways, and we carried coal from Railway Wharf to Seddons, the big salt manufacturers at Middlewich.

We now look back with great fondness on our boating years together, though I [Joyce] sometimes regret missing out on education. However, I am pleased to see all of the interest that has been generated about the canals recently.

Joyce sadly passed away in 2008.

three

Horse Power on the Canal

This is probably 'Caggy' Stevens, with a coal boat and horse at the top of the Ryder's Green locks around 1969. Notice the horse's feed tin attached to his bridle as he snacks while on the move. (D.W.)

Here we have a horse hauling rubbish at the Ryder's Flight near Great Bridge. The Eight Locks pub can be seen clearly, as can the brick hut to the left which was used as a stable. It has since been demolished.

During the generation featured within these pages – essentially the years between the 1940s and the 1970s – you will notice that many of the boatmen and women were still using horses, so this chapter deals with a brief history of how that came to be the case. The horse, with all its breeds, shapes, sizes and colours, has been essential to man's existence for thousands of years, including 200 on the narrow canals. This generally uncomplaining beast of burden, along with his four-legged cousins the mule and donkey, has been the power behind many forms of transport. Even after the introduction of steam and the internal combustion engine, horses continued to be used and valued for hauling narrow boats, through into the space age. These powerful and generally benign creatures have pulled an amazing variety of water-borne transport since Roman times.

Joe Chiltern in 1949 taking the company's materials boat to a stoppage near Lodge Farm, Netherton. The horse's driving reins can be clearly seen in this photograph. The horse was Tom.

Drawings of boat horses with a variety of craft, taken originally from a prospectus for the Forth & Clyde Canal. They appeared later in Charles Hadfield's *British Canals*. From top to bottom they illustrate: 1. Cattle and carts; 2. Coal tubs; 3. Passengers and general haulage pulled by two horses, one ridden postillion style; and 4. A swift passenger packet travelling at the fastest speed, again pulled by two horses.

Above: Horse boat *Charles*, belonging to George & Mathews of Wolverhampton, taking coal down the Staffordshire & Worcestershire Canal to Kidderminster, in the late 1940s.

Right: The same horse with Bill Tolly, stabled at New Bridge, Tettenhall, Wolverhampton.

Above: A horse with his nose in a can working up the Farmer's Bridge flight in Birmingham, in the early twentieth century. (A.E. Pratt)

Opposite above: Thomas Clayton's restored horse boat *Gifford* at Birmingham, 2003.

Opposite below: The traditions of horse boating carried on by members of the Horse Boating Society on the Grand Western Canal, 2003.

FIRKIN
FLAPPER & FIRKIN
(REGISTERED at DAVENTRY No 374)
No 60
THOS CLAYTON
1279
(OLDBURY) LIMITED
GIFFORD

Hay was brought in for feed by James Dudfield; this was the narrow boat *Dove*.

Man power

During the first half of the eighteenth century, rough gangs of men known as bow haulers had been pulling barges along rivers such as the Severn for decades, and in the process stamped out a regular trackway. However, during the last quarter of that century, various companies started to finance, construct and operate horse towing paths. So when James Brindley commenced work on the Trent & Mersey, Birmingham, and Staffordshire & Worcestershire canals, a horse towing path and the addition of facilities such as regular stabling was as important a feature of the route as the water itself. Usually one towpath was the norm, and it sat along the water-retaining embankment on sloping land. Dual towpaths appeared on a few canals only in later years with Thomas Telford on the Birmingham, and James Walker on the Tame Valley. To the best of my knowledge, only one long tunnel, the Netherton, was designed and built with a dual towpath in 1858. As a rule, horses were usually led over the top of tunnels, often by boater's children. The two short tunnels on the Staffordshire & Worcester at Dunsley and Cookley were probably Brindley's first tunnels to have a towpath.

Today, previous generations' dependence on the horse never tends to enter our consciousness, so tied are we to the operations of machinery. But to emphasise the point, when the canals were designed, they were designed around the principle of what exactly one horse could pull, and the early canal engineers did their maths. Over a pack road, one horse could carry 2cwt, but put that weight on to water, and the same animal could easily pull 25 tons. It was that simple equation that gave the impetus to the canal.

Horses, mules or donkeys?

In Britain, the horse tended to reign supreme. However, during the eighteenth century the Duke of Bridgwater, amongst others, attempted to breed mules; in fact, the first boat to travel the Duke's canal in 1761 was drawn by two mules working side by side. But as time went by, horses were preferred because they coped with cold weather that much better and, as everyone acknowledges, mules can be stubborn to the point of embarrassment. Once they have made up their mind to do their own thing, it takes great determination to dissuade them from this course, and get them back on track. This behaviour is not very helpful when you have a business to run and places to go.

Boat carriers in general were never particularly interested in the breed of horse as long as it did the job and had the temperament that allowed basic training. That said, a horse with natural intelligence was always going to be an asset, especially after learning a routine; and the horse that could go 'Bacca', a term that meant that the horse would carry on without supervision while the steerer leaned back and had a smoke, was always prized. One of the essential features of training was to get the horse used to getting a full load of 25 tons underway; this was called hauling off. It required the animal to lean forward into his collar to make a smooth transition to regular walking speed. This was not always easy in confined spaces around bridges and locks, and some horses never quite got the hang of it. A horse with a vicious or unpredictable nature was always going to be trouble and several boatmen and women were actually killed or had severe injuries from such creatures. Ill treatment was usually the other way round because the animal regularly worked a ten- to twelve-hour day, in some cases beyond its natural strength. Of course, very much depended on the policy of the canal company or, indeed, the family that operated the boat. Sensible carriers made sure that their horses were seen regularly by the blacksmith or farrier for new shoes, and that they were watered regularly and fed a mixture of hay oats and grain, though the diet was often improved with portions of vegetables.

Many horses were worked by people who were too poor or unfeeling to care for them, and they were whipped from the start of a journey to its finish, whereas more kindly families treated their animals as a respected, even loved, member of their group. Many owners were proud to show their horse off in local and national shows, and gave much attention to grooming and polished tack. Although horse deaths were common, smaller companies, and especially those that operated just one- or two-horse boats, realised that the untimely death of their horse could put them out of business. Fortunately, the treatment of horses started to improve after the first Act to prevent cruelty to horses in 1823, and later after the establishment of the RSPCA.

The twentieth century

Horse boats worked well into the twentieth century with such companies as the Anderton, T.S. Elements, Thomas Clayton, Fellows Morton & Clayton, Severn & Canal Carrying Co., plus dozens of smaller concerns. In those cases the trade was always in materials. In the previous century, horses were used to pull passenger boats known as packets, and fast boats carrying perishable commodities known as 'Fly boats'. On the Forth & Clyde Canal, packet boats carried 5,000 passengers each year. The company provided newspapers, books and games in the cabin, and even served meals and drinks. The boats completed the twenty-five miles between Glasgow and Lock 16 in five and a half hours, pulled by two horses, with the second ridden postillion. Horses were changed every two miles.

Horse trip boat at Llangollen, 2004. The company is a member of the Horse Boating Society and operates two trips per day toward the Horse Shoe Falls for much of the year.

Passengers using this service remarked that the boats were cleaner and more comfortable than the stage coaches. Fly boats on the Montgomery Canal did a regular run of thirty-two miles that included twenty-two locks, at an average speed of 6mph, which all sounds very exciting.

Today the traditions of horse boating, with all its specialised skills and expertise including care of horses and equipment, are carried on by members of the horse-boating society.

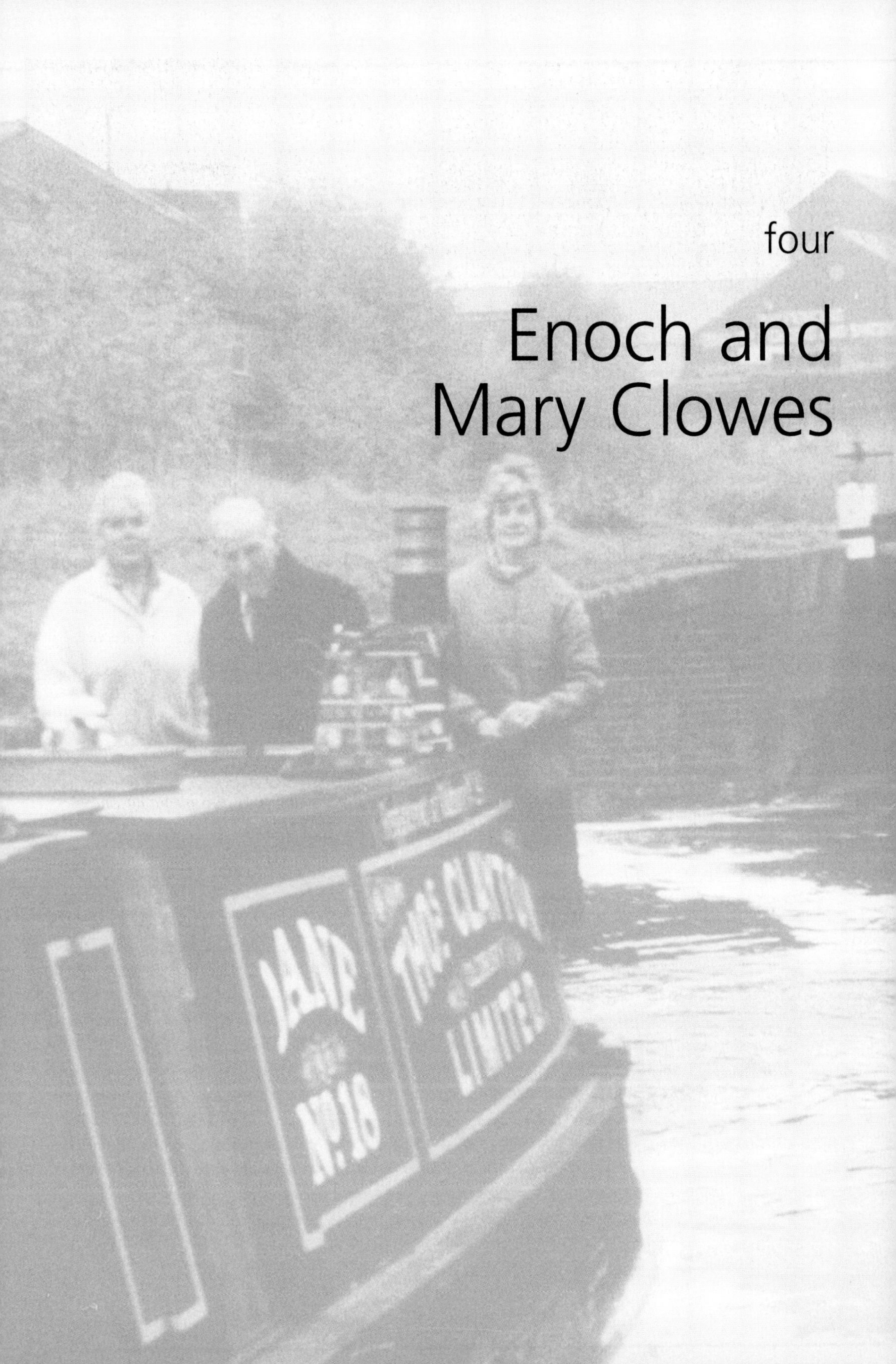

four

Enoch and Mary Clowes

Sylvia, Enoch and Mary Clowes relive their time working for Clayton's by steering the restored *Dane* down the 'Crow' or Oldbury locks.

Enoch and Mary Clowes of Oldbury talk about their births, marriage, and life on the canals, as they worked for some of the famous names of the canal-carrying era.

Enoch

When I was born on a narrow boat near Wyken, Coventry, in the December of 1919, I was the third generation of a boating family. My father and mother were Peter and Elizabeth Clowes, who had formerly worked for the Tipton firm of Fosters, but after my birth, worked for the Bedworth company of John Griffiths. During the 1920s, Griffiths operated around ten horse-drawn boats and two motor boats, and they carried anything from coal, to wheat and maize, with regular pick ups at Brentford. I happened to be the sixth in a long line of thirteen children, and even though my father was captain of two boats, pulled by one horse, the Registration of Boats Act – and of course the very limited cabin space – made it inevitable that my older siblings needed to go and work on other boats as soon as they became old enough.

Griffiths boats were of wood construction, carried up to 30 tons, and had a rear cabin with a clothed over hold. The cabin was painted black, and the white lettering read, 'John Griffiths of Bedworth'. A large chestnut horse pulled our two boats, with father steering the first, and mother the second, and we did a return trip from Brentford to Walsall in less than a week. A complete journey could take as long as three weeks. As a growing child I used to help my brother Tom work the locks, but I still had to go to school for a couple of days at

Enoch steers *Maureen* which is towing a day boat around the tight turn onto the Old Main Line above Brades locks, Oldbury. They are heading for Albright & Wilson's factory to collect another load of highly toxic phosphorous waste. In better times, Matty's cabin sides were painted a bright acid yellow with black lettering that read 'Alfred Matty & Sons'.

Brentford. This was a special school for us boat kids, and there were two classes. I remember having two note books, and my teachers were Miss Baker and Miss Moore.

During the 1930s, father had changed employment to the much bigger company of Fellows, Morton & Clayton, and our base was the Fazeley Street depot in Birmingham. I was now helping to cloth up the boat and keep it clean, and for these jobs dad gave me two pence a week, which I used to save up to go to the pictures.

My bed was a thin mattress, rolled up and stored away during the day, and then it came out in the evening to fit along the side of the cabin. For breakfast, we might have toast and marmalade, or even egg and bacon. Some years later, working for FMC during the war years, we had a regular run when we loaded up with empty anti aircraft shells from the Prothero tube works in Wednesbury. We took them down to London, on the Grand Union Canal. This entailed a final leg along the Thames to Woolwich Arsenal. For the return journey we would load up with groceries from City road, and bring them back to Birmingham. For some reason that I can't now recall, I went off one day to enrol in the services. However, I was later informed that I was doing a necessary job, and couldn't be spared from boating; it was important war work. But I still hankered for the excitement of a uniform, so I talked my friend George Berrol into letting me wear his when we went into town. Unfortunately, one of his officers spotted us, and poor old Berrol had to peel potatoes for quite some time.

The heavy work of loading and unloading the boats by hand continued, and my father said one day that even though the work was killing him, it wasn't going to kill me, so he took the job of captain, with Thomas Clayton of Oldbury. Clayton's boats were flat-topped tank boats that usually carried a liquid cargo that was either pumped in or out. This saved all the heavy handballing of goods, and our first boats were *Brent* and *Cherwell*.

At the age of twenty, I also started with the firm as a captain, assisted by Tom, and my first boat was the *Erewash* – all of Clayton's boats were named after rivers. We had a small Arabian mare named Bett who wasn't really up to the job, but even worse she had a stubborn contrary nature, and would show her displeasure by putting her ears back. One day she kicked me hard, breaking my arm, and knocking my teeth though my lip. I decided that it was high time to have a new horse, and we had Betty, a lovely tempered big chestnut. She adored being groomed, which was a daily chore, and the firm supplied curry combs and dandy brushes for this task. I then went onto the Ellesmere Port run, bringing back oil to Oldbury. Later I changed from the *Erewash* to the *Hebble*. I got to see Mary occasionally because her mother and father also worked for Clayton's. She was five years younger than me, and one of nine children. They were big families in those days.

Mary

My family, too, were working a couple of Clayton's boats during these years, the *Hamble*, and the *Pinn*, and, like Enoch's family we were on the weekly run up the Shropshire Union Canal from Oldbury to Ellesmere Port and back. As a young girl my mother taught me to cook using the small black coal fired Signora range, and I learned to cook complete dinners and stews. The coal was kept in the coal drawer, which doubled as a step down into the cabin. I vividly recall my mom as being a strong and capable woman, but she was also very kind, and was always ready to go and help any of the other boating families, especially if the mothers were in labour. It wasn't always possible to get hold of a midwife when you were in the middle of the countryside, and babies never come to schedule anyway, so mom often had to help out, as other women helped her, in her time of need.

My mom loved looking after the two horses, and a regular treat for them was getting one of Thorley's Powders. These fine brown powders that came in little packets were supplied by the company, but you could also buy them at the canal shops. Sprinkled onto their feed, they were a kind of tonic, and they had one every three or four days. The horses loved them. Occasionally a horse came down with colic, a type of acute stomach pain that would make them fall down on their side. We would then have to send for the vet, who would pour a revolting brown liquid into what was known as a drenching horn. A drenching horn was, in fact, a cow's horn used to get the medicine down the animal's throat, after pushing his tongue to one side with a twitch, a stick and rope device.

Dad was a real happy-go-lucky individual whose simple pleasure was going for a pint, and when I started to go seriously with Enoch, he sometimes took him along. I was now seventeen, Enoch was twenty-two, and even though we literally only saw each other like literal passing ships in the night on our journeys up and down the Shroppie, our moorings and unloading did sometimes coincide, which gave us time to talk and make our plans for the future. We married in 1944 at Oldbury parish church, and my few personal effects, including my plates and brass rods for the range, went onto the *Hebble*.

Enoch

Being married and captain of my own boat was marvellously liberating, but our daily routine was unchanged since we were still doing the same runs to Ellesmere Port and back. Getting to the Shellmex depot to load up entailed a two-mile trip along the Manchester Ship Canal, towed always in twos by a tug, while our horse was left at the stable. Once alongside the depot, the oil was pumped into the boat via the central deck hatch, and then we were on our return journey. My pay at the end of the war, as a newly married man, was £4 10*s* for a round trip, but you didn't get this all at once. When you set out from Clayton's base, which is situated on the Old Main Line near Oldbury, you were given £3, and then on your return you received the rest – £1 10*s*. This was known as 'settling up'. Harry Clayton was the boss in those days, but a Mr Craddock was the man that we saw most. He was responsible for giving us our orders and paying out our wages, and he was there at the office till eight o'clock at night.

One day I had a loaded boat that was destined for Bilston, and as usual Mr Craddock gave me my start money. But when I gave Tom his 30 bob, I realised that there was £6 in the packet – £3 too much. So when I came back I asked Mr Craddock if he was any money short, and I explained that he must have made the mistake of putting it into my packet. Instead of taking it back he simply said, 'You're honest. You keep it'. I asked him if he was sure, and he simply told me to put it back in my pocket, and he walked away In 1946, our first child Sylvia was born – yes, on the boat and not far from the oiling up shed – as she often reminds us. But as the *Hebble* was a small boat, only fit for two people, the company moved us on to the *Oka*.

Mary

This was the iron that I used for the clothes in those days. [Mary produced a small cast-iron device that looked hundreds of years old.] The iron went onto the top of the stove to get really hot; meanwhile I would lower the cupboard door that doubled as a dining table and ironing board. Living, cooking, eating and sleeping in a space of only 10ft by 7 was an art, and many items had several purposes. It was our way of life, and I had never known anything different. The iron could get a dirty sole sitting on the range, so most people had a chrome plate attachment with springs that clipped onto the bottom of the iron, thus keeping your clothes clean. Some families had two irons; this meant that you could be using one, while reheating the second. During the years following the war we were still using horse-drawn boats, and Sylvia, and later her brother, loved to ride on the back of our horse, though they had to remember to 'duck' at the bridges. A later horse called Ginger Bob was so attached to us that he thought that he was one of the family. This caused a problem one day when he pulled his stake out of the ground and followed Enoch down to the shop. Fortunately, the policeman was a reasonable man and looked after him while Enoch went in and purchased his groceries.

Enoch

Another of our regular trips was to Majors of Wolverhampton near Monmore Green, where we used to load up with creosote. Majors was a tar works, and we would then deliver to

Four Ashes, on the Staffordshire & Worcestershire Canal. It was on one of those runs that I was forced to moor up at the top of the Wolverhampton 21. This was because Mary was about to give birth to our son.

Much of Clayton's work was bound up with the Midlands gas works, and the substances that were made as a by-product of manufacturing town gas. A regular short run commenced by picking up two loads of tar from Swan Village gas works (West Bromwich) and bringing this along the Wednesbury Old Canal to Oldbury tar works, at the bottom of the Oldbury locks or 'The Crow' as we called it. Then later in the day, we transported tar water from there to Robinsons Chemicals at Ryder's Green Junction. There were of course many runs to distant gas works, and my brother Albert boated tar from Leamington to our base at Oldbury.

I finished with Clayton's about 1957. Many of the gas works were closing as North Sea Gas started to take the place of manufactured gas, and thus that work came to an end, so I went boating at Alfred Matty's. They had an office in Gate Street near Burnt Tree, Dudley, but they soon moved to a second bigger yard off Biddings Lane, Coseley. This was right on the Wolverhampton Main Line Canal. The yard had originally been a coal yard owned by Jim Wright, but now Matty's were using it for a base that had regular contracts with Albright & Wilson, a big Oldbury chemical firm. The open boat I now had, fitted with a Bollinder, was named *Maureen*, and it towed a butty. My new, but hazardous, job was to transport effluent waste, and sometimes phosphorus, to a dumping site near the junction with the Netherton branch canal. Thankfully, Mary and I were now living in a house.

The huge marl hole that served us as a waste dump had many years before been the site of the Rattlechain brick works, and also the place where a disastrous breach of the canal had occurred late in the nineteenth century. But now there was just this enormous marl hole, filled with the most horrid blue water in which nothing could live. And it was this ghastly cargo that nearly finished me and my mate off one day. We arrived at the dumping site, and started the petrol Meadows pump to empty the boat. Within minutes the pump stopped working, and as we tried to sort the problem out we were both overcome by the toxic fumes coming from the outlet pipe. Fortunately, a passer-by helped us to safety, and Frank Matty told us to take a few days off to get over it. That's how it was in those days. I carried on with that job at Matty's until I finally left the canals in 1970 for a land-based job with Albright & Wilson's that lasted until my retirement. I am now eighty-one, and Mary and I still look with great fondness on our life together on the cut.

Horse boat passing Ocker Hill power station. (D.W.)

14 June 1965. Alfred Matty boats were at one time based in Gate Street Tipton, and a slipway near Willenhall, but moved to a yard near Deepfields Junction, Coseley. Enoch Clowes is at the tiller of the motor boat *Maureen* at Brades locks, Oldbury. Ocker Hill power station is in the distance. (D.W.)

five

Maureen Shaw of Middlewich

Maureen at the tiller of Thomas Clayton's *Pinn* at Chemistry Lock, Chester, on the Shropshire Union Canal.

Maureen

It is a not an easy admission to make to oneself, let alone to a national readership, that as a child it seems that my mother couldn't keep me. Her relationship with her husband had broken down, she was on her own, and I was a burden to her. So one evening, when I was about two, she went into the pub to talk to Danny Jinks, a boatman, who she knew, and asked him if he would take me off her hands. I have been told that her actual words were, 'Will you take this wench off me?'.

Danny and his wife Nellie had recently lost their first baby in childbirth, and the hope of having more babies was by no means certain. My mother must have thought that handing me over to them was a good thing for both parties, but Danny's wife Nellie was not at first pleased with the decision that her husband had made, and told him that she didn't want someone else's throw out. Fortunately for me he must have convinced her, and I am very glad that he did. Nellie went on to have children of her own, but I'm glad to say that the Jinks loved and cared for me as one of their own, and I have always referred to them as mom and dad.

Before Nellie married Danny she had been in service at a big house, and while there she had received something of an education, which was rare for boat people during the 1920s and '30s. Danny had previously worked on the fly boats, but when I was growing up along with John, Violet, Mary, and Nellie (junior), they boated for Thomas Clayton's of Oldbury. Their yard, with its blacksmiths, stables and offices was always a busy spot, with their flat-topped tank boats coming and going at all hours of the day and night. Some things stick in your mind, and I remember that there was red carpet in the offices, and the boss's Jag and Bentley were usually parked outside.

Opposite bottom: A fine gathering of boating families on Rayner's boats at Runcorn, probably during the 1930s.

Right: Maureen Shaw at Wardle Lock, Middlewich, 2001.

Below: Jack Shaw operates the windlass of a spoon dredger whilst Frank Lyons handles the 'spoon' itself. Jack' assistant has, sadly, been obliterated from the photograph as a result of poor storage.

Potter & Sons' boats at the Anderton lift with Tom and Aggie Barber. The house belonging to the lift operator is in the background.

Manchester top lock in the 1930s, with the lock house and viaduct in the background.

The yard man was named Dicky Gibbs, his house was also off the boatyard, and I also recall the tragic year that his daughter died after falling from the step.

As a young girl I was taught how to steer the boat and drive the horse, and I must have clocked up hundreds of miles on foot as I followed those four powerful plodding hooves along the Oxford and Grand Union canals. From Clayton's base on the Old Main Line (Wolverhampton–Birmingham) at Oldbury, we did many of the southern routes down to Banbury and Oxford, or to Leamington

Spa, delivering or collecting from the gas works in those towns. There was considerable traffic on the canals in the years before and during World War Two, and there was much competition to get into the locks from companies like Barlow's and the Grand Union boats.

I recall one winter vividly, for many boats were frozen up near Napton Junction for roughly seven weeks. The ice boats tried to get through, but the water, especially in the locks, had frozen to a formidable depth, and their brave attempts failed. Fortunately the 'Ovalteeners' as we called them, shared their cargoes with us so that we could make hot drinks, and the Barlow's boatmen gave us coal for the ranges. Napton hill, with its windmill and the surrounding fields, looked very pretty clad in snow, but the mothers became increasingly anxious as each week went by as to how they were going to feed their children. Some of us went to work on the nearby farm, and we were rewarded not with money, but with bacon and eggs – just as good a payment I'm sure you will agree. Mr Thomas Clayton, the big boss, even came out one day to give us money to buy corn for the horse, and that gesture will give you an indication for whom or what came first. Yes, your horse was a valued and well-looked-after commodity, but to the company, an important asset.

As a youngster I used to daydream about living in a house and going to school to get educated, and occasionally we spent a few precious days at either St Mary's Wolverhampton or at Ellesmere Port, when we were on the Shroppie runs. But I remember well the continual rivalry between the 'townies' and us boat children. The townies would move away from us if we sat near them on the same bench and they made rude comments about us washing in the canal – though of course we never did. There were regular fights. However, there were some townies that we mixed with. They gave us comics to look at, and we gave them rope for skipping – it seemed a fair exchange at the time. Back on the boat, every child had their chores to do, which included washing the boat down, polishing brasses or assisting with the preparation and cooking of meals. Once, a lady in a posh tweed suit and a feather in her hat came to us on the towpath, and questioned us kids about whether we had had a bath, or if we had been beaten lately. She must have been satisfied with our answers, because all she said to mom was, 'You're doing a good job, keep it up'.

Eventually, the company changed over from horses to motor boats, and we took on the Spey, along with a butty. However, dad, with his corduroy trousers and cap, was a very placid man and could never seem to get the hang of using an engine, so to help out we had a young man named Harry Powell come along as mate. I liked Harry because he used to read to us. Mom was of small stature, but being a strong personality she was the real boss of the family, and she taught me such important principles as never to tell a lie, and never to borrow from others.

It was mom who dealt with the finances, and one day Danny came across the yard with a pay-packet that was 10*s* short – a lot of money in those days. She went over the details as usual with a pencil on a sugar packet, and then armed with the evidence, she sent Danny to confront Mr Craddock, who was in charge of the wages. When he saw him approach he said, 'Are you still here Danny?', who replied, 'My Nellie says I'm 10*s* short', at which Mr Craddock replied that if there were many more like his Nellie, he would become bankrupt, and he threw the 10*s* note at him.

At the age of fourteen I became due for my employment card, and Nellie thought that it was time that I learned the truth of my first few years of life, of my real mother, and how she and Danny came to have me. To verify her story, and enable me to get my card, she handed me my grubby birth certificate.

Two years later I was married to John Shaw at Broad Street (Wolverhampton) registry office, though everyone called him Jack. He was working for Fellows Morton & Clayton, and we had become familiar with each other from boating the Shropshire Union. World

Danny and Nellie Jinks with Harry Powel at the rear, and a young John Jinks, on the Willow Wren boat *Irlam*.

War Two had been over for five years, but rationing of certain foods and other items was still going on, and I am glad that I kept all my ration books as mementos. John was captain of the *Dace* but I found the routine of an FMC boat very different to that of Claytoning, and to be honest I wasn't too keen. My reasons were that there was never any clothing up to do on the oil boats, and every time I ran along the top planks or tried to tie up the ropes on *Dace*, I nearly fell in. Cargoes for FMC were constantly changing and included all kinds of goods such as sugar from Tate & Lyle at Ellesmere Port, flour from Sun Mills and cocoa beans. These goods came south along the Shroppie and were unloaded right in the heart of Birmingham. Metal tubes, and sometimes spelter, went the other way.

Young men were still being called into the army to do their stint of national service, and I had to go back with mom and dad on the *Spey* and the *Pinn* while Jack did his two years. After that we did some work for Clayton's before I left the canals and Jack transferred to 'The Company' as the relatively new British Waterways was called. The carrying days were now almost over, and Jack's work was on the spoon dredger, which was a very hard way of getting the muck off the canal bed. We used to say that it was the only way of stopping the bottom from getting too near the top.

Ironically, as I head toward my sixty-eighth birthday, I am having more contact with the canals than the last twenty years put together. For since Jack died six years ago, I have been giving talks all over the country following a boat show in London, when I did a radio interview with Cliff Mitchelmore. At the show, the organisers had built a full-size model of the lock cottage that we lived in at Middlewich, complete with lock and narrow boat. It was quite a feat, and attracted considerable attention. Thankfully, my mind and memory are still sharp, even though I never did learn to read and write, and I shall go on relating our tales of a working life on the canal for as long as I am able.

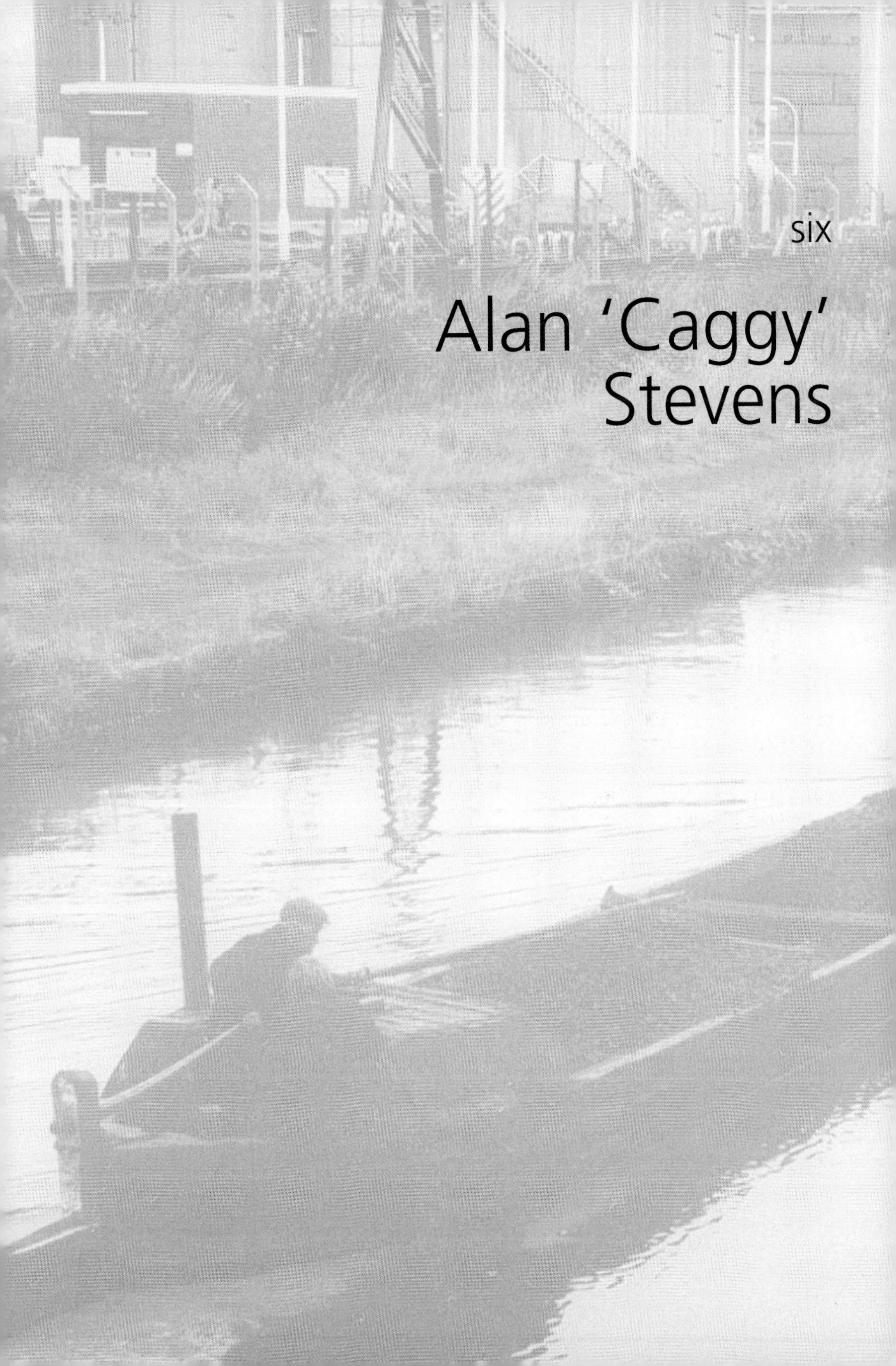

six

Alan 'Caggy' Stevens

There is no doubt in my mind that the name of 'Caggy' Stevens, christened Alan in 1919, should be engraved in the Guinness Book of Records *in several categories. Probably the most outstanding of those achievements would be for keeping the skill of horse boating alive way into the 1990s. Jeff Bennet, who worked with 'Caggy' for many years, assisted him on regular narrow boat trips around the BCN, taking school parties and pensioners. However, this use of the horse for motive power was in one very important way unlike the occasional horse-boating trips undertaken by historic or leisure operators. Rather, this was an extension of 'Caggy's' boating expertise and business diversification. He had the canny ability to adapt and survive the great changes in transport that had occurred during his lifetime in the twentieth century.*

In the 1930s Alan followed his father onto the canals, working on the big coal haulage contracts that were to remain viable up to and after the Second World War. Following the end of that conflict, coal was still transported by canal to power stations and coal merchants, but its use in industry and domestic fire grates was dwindling fast. It was during the years 1940–1960 that dozens of canal operators sold their boats, closed their yards and moved on to pastures new. Wharves that had been vibrant with the sounds and activities of the daily loading and unloading of motors and their butties were now as silent as the grave. The once-lucrative work of general goods carrying was long gone, but 'Caggy', who was naturally endowed with a spirit of tenacity and determination, but above all a willingness to spend long hours on the canal in all weathers, would discover the tiniest of niches and continue.

So, what work was there left? Well after the war there was still a little coal coming out of the local pits, and he worked alongside other small operators like Leonard Leigh, Ernest Thomas and of course T.S. Elements of Oldbury, where he always stabled his horse. Also, 'Caggy' has the distinction of bringing the last horse-drawn boat from the Cannock collieries.

Then there was dredging and rubbish removal. Factories in and around Birmingham produced tons of rubbish, and 'Caggy' had regular runs into places like Raleigh, United Wire and Pierce & Cutler, collecting their rubbish and taking it to the tip at Moxley on the Walsall Canal.

Opposite above: Superb study of 'Caggy' with 'Mac' and an open boat. (*Birmingham Post & Mail*)

Opposite below: Disaster at Great Bridge, December 1966. The horse 'Candy' was spooked by a nearby compressor and went into the canal. This particular tale had a sad ending because, after the arrival of the vet, it was deemed best to put the animal down, which was an expensive and upsetting experience for all. (D.W.)

In the late 1970s, after he had moved into the yard at Tipton, he hired out open boats to contractors who were doing canal maintenance work, bridge repairs, and the laying of miles of gas mains under the towpath. All these little jobs added up, keeping 'Caggy', and his one or two assistants, gainfully employed. As I mentioned before, Jeff Bennet worked with him for years, and then in 1992 Ralph Miles started at the Tipton Yard, and still operates there today with boat building, repairs and hire.

Brades locks, Oldbury, 31 December 1966. George Boddley, who previously worked for Clayton's, is leading the horse along a treacherous winter towpath. The boat probably belongs to T.S. Elements.

Right: A couple of 'Caggy's' old day boats still hanging about his old yard in 2002.

Opposite above: 'Caggy's' rubbish boat being operated by Geoff Bennet down the Birmingham 13. He also operated the tug *Caggy* – well, what else? – and about six open boats that included the *Lyn*, *Joey* and *Arthur*. (G. Bennet)

Opposite below: 29 July 1967. 'Caggy', on the opposite towpath, driving the horse along the main line near West Bromwich. Jack Smith has the tiller as they haul coal in a leaking Leonard Leigh boat. A petrol pump has been fitted to stop them sinking. (D.W.)

In 1973 a local writer named Vivian Bird spent a day with 'Caggy', and I quote from his book Staffordshire:

I met Caggy on a drizzling cloud-wrack of a July dawn at Whimsey Bridge, Oldbury. He was harnessing his dappled roan 'Mac' to a towline, and soon the open boat 'Trigo' was gliding gently up the cut, bound empty for Cannock coal field, where it would be left for filling, while Mac hauled back another of Caggy's boats, already loaded with 24 tons of coal for a Birmingham factory. I took the tiller, and as the light strengthened, Caggy could be seen stepping out smartly with Mac, easing the towrope over obstacles. Beneath the bridges Mac's otherwise silent tread echoed a loud Clip-clop on the tarmac, but as we turned from the high level to the low at Brades Hall Junction, his muzzle was removed and he munched white clover during pauses in dropping down the three locks into a ravaged landscape of jagged rubbish tips, smoking chimneys, and white flowered Elder bushes.

From the Eight Locks pub in Ryder's Green road, we dropped down eight locks to Great Bridge. In the last pound, Caggy pointed out a wooden stump with a 'D' inscribed on it and explained; 'That's a distance post. If yo'r oss ad reached it gooin up, yo could claim right 'o' way into lock seven against a boat comin down. A boat lockin down could claim lock eight if its oss were under Brickhouse Lane Bridge'.

Fifteen tethering rings in a wall near the bottom lock bear witness to the horse drawn heyday of canals. Once past the pools of the derelict railway basin at Great Bridge, we entered a sulphurous smell near Hempole Lane Bridge, to turn right beneath the three huge bobbins of 'Ocker Bonk' power station, at the Tame Valley Junction, where the canal was unencumbered enough for a spell of 'backering'. 'Backering' said Caggy, settling on the cabin roof, 'that's when the oss goes on with us resting on the boat. Mac's a good backerin oss, an ideal boat oss, light legged, and eats and sleeps well. Cost me £110 from Birmingham Corporation.'

Working up the 'Gansey' the first seven locks on the Rushall canal, Caggy remembered some canal characters. 'There was "Nine Lives" who helped kill a thief on the towpath with a tiller; Bill Taylor from Oldbury – very fast, yo do arf av to move if he wor behind you; Stabbit and Starchy, old Brummagem chaps; and old "Drown the boat, who sank his boat in Perry Barr top lock and got three months."'

Surprising statistics have stuck in Caggy's head, too. 'On good Friday, 1937,' he said, '80 boats loaded with coal and slack came down Rushall locks. Today not half a dozen working boats ply the canal.' On we glided, the canal curving high above Dumble Derry, an open space where a strong wind plays havoc with a light empty boat, so that in Caggy's inimitable words – 'We have to trot we oss.'

Opposite the old Walsall Wood Colliery, Caggy pointed out a small brick building. 'That was a hovel' he said. 'The canal companies built hovels for boatmen without cabins. I've often slep in em on a bag 'o' corn. At Benny's at Little Bloxwich, we once ad an oss in as well. Them wer rough days. If yo cor fight yo wornt in the team'.

Walsall Wood church and a neat cricket ground passed below us. 'When fust I come up here' said Caggy 'The ground was level with the canal. Now through mining it's sunk about ten feet.' Turning into the Wyrley & Essington canal at Catshill, we finally reached our destination. The canal, milky at Oldbury, smoking with phosphorous at Tipton, bottle green at West Bromwich, and weedy at Rushall, was now deep and crystal clear. With the Chasewater reservoir dam half a mile ahead, and with reference to no one, we tied up 'Trigo', moved our belongings to boat No 1,297, already filled with coal, harnessed up the faithful 'Mac' and started back the way we had come.

Yes, 'Caggy' was very much a product of the Black Country, just like its coal and iron, a distinctive character on the Birmingham canals with his check shirt, braces, corduroy trousers, and of course his battered trilby hat. His intimate knowledge of the Black Country canals came from decades of using Shank's Pony, and it was suitably matched by his lifelong association with one of man's best friends, the horse. (Using Shank's Pony is a Black Country term for walking. A whimsy was a winding machine at collieries.)

seven

Charlie and Ellen Harris

Charles and Ellen Harris relate their experiences when they worked for the Severn and Canal Carrying Co., and the Grand Union Canal Carrying Co.

Charlie Harris, born October 1922

I spent the large part of my early life afloat, but my earliest memories are of the journey along the Severn River from Gloucester docks to Worcester, and then up the Worcester & Birmingham Canal to the industrial Midlands or beyond. As children, I and my younger brother Arthur used to hang out from the moving boat with a stick collecting leaves from the water's surface, then when we were a little older, dad eased us into the usual jobs of running a narrow boat. To give me a bit of height, he would put a sack of corn in the hatches so that I could stand on it and see over the cabin to steer. My father's name was George, and though he had worked for the firm of Smarts of Chelford before I was born, I only remember him working for the Severn & Canal Carrying Co., which we simply referred to as the 'Severner's'. The contrast between those two carriers couldn't have been greater, for Smarts was a coal and timber merchants with one boat, pulled by the two donkeys, Jinny and Billy, while the Severner's was a whole fleet of nearly 100 boats that included 70ft narrow boats, river barges, tugs, trows and one coaster. As the name Severner's implies, the company's carrying work centred on the river Severn, plus the major ports in its estuarial waters like Swansea, Newport and Bristol, but its collections and deliveries branched out into many of the other inland waterways that connected with that vibrant busy river.

My father's and mother's home was the cabin of the *Wilden*, a timber boat built by the company at its Stourport yard in 1924, two years after my birth. Incidentally, Wilden is an area not far from Stourport. The livery, like all the other Severner's boats, was two distinctive shades of light and dark blue, with white lettering (early lettering was with aluminium letters). The narrow boats were always clothed over, and the company's name continued along the tarpaulins from the front to the rear. During the 1930s, Gloucester docks, with its enormous warehouses, was a bustling and exciting port for a child to be in, with a mix of ocean-going vessels bringing in raw materials from exotic countries, transhipping to smaller river craft and narrow boats like ours, all lashed together in rows. After being loaded at Gloucester, a whole host of narrow boats would be tied nose to tail, in pairs, and hauled by one of the company's tugs the twenty-eight miles to Diglis locks at Worcester, with the halfway point at Tewkesbury. From the Diglis locks that connects the Severn with the canal, we were then on our own in the relatively still and safe waters of the Birmingham & Worcester Canal, pulled steadily onward and ever upward those fifty eight locks by one of the company's many horses. The lock keeper at Diglis was a Danny Watton, and close to the locks were the company's stables run by Bert Mon, with room for about twenty animals. We would also collect sacks of corn for our animals at this point, though the company also had other smaller stables halfway up the locks and at Tardebigge.

Opposite below, left: Nellie's mother Sarah Harris perched on the GUCCCo butty *Ruislip* during the Second World War at Hatton locks. Behind is her second husband Harry Harris on the motor boat *Reading*. The boats are carrying cement on a regular run from Southam to Camp Hill in Birmingham. Nellie is off, no doubt, working the lock.

Opposite below, right: A young Arthur Harris taking *Wilden*'s horse over the top of Tardebigge tunnel. The muzzle was to stop the horse from constantly grazing.

Above: Nellie and Charlie at a celebration dinner in 2001.

Left: Severn & Canal Carrying Co.'s horse boat *Wilden* with, from left to right: Terry Palin, Arthur Harris and his brother Charlie Harris, aged about fourteen. In the background is Llanthony Warehouse, now the Waterways Museum at Gloucester.

Below: Steam tug *Primrose* around 1940, prior to conversion to diesel on the Gloucester & Sharpness Canal.

Opposite: Severn & Canal Carrying Co.'s letterhead to Charlie.

ALL COMMUNICATIONS TO BE ADDRESSED TO THE COMPANY

SEVERN CARRYING COMPANY LTD.

TELEPHONE MIDLAND 4061 (3 LINES. P.B.EX) TELEGRAMS "SEVERN, BIRMINGHAM"

CARRIERS BY WATER BETWEEN Birmingham & Wolverhampton Districts and The Bristol Channel Ports

IN REPLY PLEASE QUOTE OUR REF. .... YOUR REF. ....

HEAD OFFICE 16 BRIDGE STREET · BROAD STREET BIRMINGHAM·1 16th.September 1944

14600631 Spr. Harris C.H.,
Richard Ward,
North Field,
Military Hospital,
BIRMINGHAM, 31.

Dear Sir,

In reply to your letter of August 8th., if you are successful in getting your discharge from the Army, and your previous employers, The Sharpness Docks Co. do not want to take you back, will you please call at our Office and see Mr. F.Trigg, who will try and arrange it with the Ministry of Labour for you to be sent to work for us - if you are physically fit.

Yours faithfully,
For SEVERN CARRYING CO. LTD.,

General Manager.

B/R/B.

There were also several watering points along the route because the water in the canal was extremely saline from Stoke Works down, probably due to the high salt content in the Droitwich area, or maybe from the salt works itself. The salt run was done by Danny and Jack Merril from Stoke Works into Birmingham, while matches from England's Glory at Gloucester were transported by Charles Ballinger.

Our next boats were the motor boat *No.8*, which Arthur and I worked while dad used the horse boat *Sharpness*. It was always good to arrive at Tardebigge top lock for the views were marvellous. This was also the place to leave our horse behind. We were now on the summit pound leading to either Bournville or Birmingham, and our motor boat now towed the butty for the rest of the journey. One of the interesting features of this journey was watching the tug boats at work, of which there were three. This was due to the fact there are no towpaths in the tunnels along the Birmingham & Worcester. The first tug, the *Worcester*, would haul the horse boats through the Tardebigge and Shortwood tunnels at 6 a.m., and then they would be taken through the Wast Hill tunnel (we always knew this as the Kings Norton tunnel) by the tug *Birmingham* or *Gloucester* and pick up their horses at the other end. The horses followed the paths over the top; often they would be ridden by the younger members of the family, but it's safe to say that it was the horses that knew the way best.

At Dunhampstead tunnel, though, there was a different procedure. This tunnel, about a mile from Hanbury wharf, is only 236 yards long, and the practice was to send the horse over the top. Meanwhile, the boatman hand pulled his boat through the tunnel by means of the rails fitted to the tunnel walls. Whoever took the horse over the top would, on arrival at the other end, dangle the rope into the tunnel mouth, anchoring it by a large metal weight. Then as the boat came through, it was easy for the skipper to grab the rope, put it back on the mast and be away again.

Ellen (Nellie) Harris, born December 1924

In 1934, when I was ten, my mother remarried a Mr Harry Harris, who was then working for the Sevener's, and we joined him on his horse boat, doing similar journeys as Charlie, i.e. from Bristol to Sharpness. When I was thirteen, my stepfather changed companies, and we transferred to the Grand Union Canal Carrying Co. For a short time we had the two Town Class boats *Reading* and *Ruislip*, and later the *Halsall* and *Regulus*. The first two were iron boats; the *Reading* being the motor boat, with an 18hp National engine, towing *Ruislip*, the butty. At that time quite a few boaters from the Gloucester area also moved to the GUCCCo., including the names of Best, Hopkins and Cannon.

The depot that we were based at was Bulls Bridge, West London, four miles out of Brentford, right on the junction of the Paddington Arm and the Grand Union Canal. At Bulls Bridge we used to get our orders, and also fill up with diesel. Many of our collection points were from the Limehouse Docks on the Regents Canal near the Thames, where we usually loaded with steel. While dad was loading up, I would sometimes on a Sunday take the bus to Petticoat Lane and treat myself to maybe chocolates, or some new stockings, and then it was back to the boat. I was fortunate to have the cabin of the motor boat all to myself, while mom and dad slept in the butty.

Oak graining decorated the inside of the cabin, while brass rods and a bit of crochet work made it a little more homely. Most other boats were still lit at night by paraffin lamps, but all GUCCCo. boats had been improved by the addition of a generator, battery, and internal lighting. It was a 12V system that worked extremely well, also powering a useful headlamp, which made travelling at night that much easier.

Sometimes we went to the Victoria Docks near Greenwich to pick up wheat. This meant that we had to take on a pilot at Limehouse, to navigate the tricky waters of the Thames. From there, it was a long journey back up the Grand Union to Leicester, or further on up the river Soar to Loughborough or Nottingham. At Foxton locks my mother would probably buy provisions from the lock keeper. This could easily include a fowl which she would pluck during the day, and later cook it for dinner. This was just one of the many miscellaneous tasks that my mother had to perform during a day's work. It was amazing how much she did, and I'll never now how she managed it all. There was a fully laden boat to steer and manoeuvre in and out of locks, with all of the rope work that that entailed, as well as the usual wifely chores of cooking, washing and keeping home. In the summer, our working days were long indeed, and on occasions dad would get us started just after midnight to improve his pay. Boatmen at that time were paid by the tonnage that they delivered, not by the hours they worked. At Nottingham we might pick up ceramic pipes, or maybe coal from Langley Mill, which was delivered to London. All coal was shovelled out by hand. When I was a teenager most of my work was lock wheeling, and I used a bicycle to help me get about. We also did regular cement runs form Southam up to Camp Hill in Birmingham.

Even though this material was bagged, cement was still dreadful stuff to handle, and the fine powder seemed to get in every nook and cranny. Just like Charlie, we also endured weeks of being frozen in and unable to get any work done, and the worst year in my memory was 1939. The following war years also brought their own dangers, and once when we were on the Regents Canal, the German bombers came over to inflict as much damage as possible on the docks, and we weren't far away. The sound of multiple explosions and red glows coming over the top of the buildings was an experience I could well do without. Charlie and I celebrated VJ Day and VE Day along with thousands of others in Gloucester when the war came to an end. Though Charlie and I had known each other as youngsters working for the Severner's, we came into contact with each other again towards the end of the war, thanks to a little match-making from mother. We started off by going to the cinema together; our relationship grew from these outings, and we were married in June 1945.

Charlie, and horse boating skills

Of course, many of the skills of horse boating have been lost, but there was one lock procedure that we regularly used to help the animals get loaded boats out of the lock with less effort. A running block was attached to the mast, and the towing line from the horse passed through this block and back to a metal pin at the top of the lock landing. This meant in practice that the horse now had a mechanical advantage, and pulled with the power of two. The boat quickly gained speed as we left the lock, and as a wooden pin fixed in the line ran up to the block, the line stopped, and the horse again took on the full weight of the boat. Then as the boat passed the metal pin, the loop in the rope simply slipped off, and we were bound for the next lock. It always amazed me how clever the horses were because they always used to come back to the boat as soon as it was in the lock so that the line could be run through to the pin – clever creatures really if you looked after them.

During the first winter of the war I remember being frozen up at Barbridge Junction on the Shropshire Union Canal, along with several other boats. At that time I was on the Ash with Harry Price the skipper. After picking up a load of wheat at Ellesmere Port, we were bound for the mill at the top of the Wolverhampton locks. Our boat was completely frozen up for around eight weeks, along with some FMC boats including Reg Price in the *Swan*, Jack Stokes in *Bromsgrove* and Billy Helms on motor boat *No.7*. Fortunately, I was just old enough to sign on, and we walked along crisp towpaths into Nantwich to get our money. In those days labour money was 6*s* per week.

The company carried all kinds of freight that included chocolate for Cadbury's, fruit, sugar, Typhoo tea, wheat, spelter, copper and aluminium, and there were many cargoes of cardboard to Blackpole, a few miles north of Worcester. Cadbury's, as you probably know, is one of the largest manufactures of chocolate in the world, and though they have several works around the country including Frampton (Gloucester & Sharpness Canal) and Knighton (Shropshire Union Canal), their main place was at Bournville, a few miles south of Birmingham. The Bournville factory and the housing for its workers had been conveniently sited alongside the Worcester & Birmingham Canal in 1879 by the brothers Richard and George Cadbury.

In the early 1900s the company had expanded greatly and at one time they ran their own fleet of narrow boats, carrying milk and raw materials to the factories, but by the 1930s their distinctive maroon boats had been taken over by the Severner's, who were now doing most of their transport. (T&S Elements delivered their coal.) Cargoes for Cadbury's included a stuff called 'Mass'; this was made from cocoa beans that had been ground and formed into large rough lumps, then put into sacks. Many tons of this Mass was boated from Bournville

A typical BCN post, now the symbol of the BCN Society.

to Frampton, while chocolate crumb – a mix of cocoa, sugar and concentrated milk – was unloaded at Bournville. To cater for this extensive trade, Cadbury's had their own wharf at the side of the canal and I remember it well. Enormous open sheds towered over the towpath so that the valuable cargoes could be kept dry, while many pairs of boats were unloaded by crane onto the waiting trucks. Cadbury's also had their own internal railway system, with the trucks beautifully signwritten in the company's colours and lettering.

The following year, 1940, I went to work for the Gloucester & Sharpness Co. as a fireman on their tugs. These boats were steam-driven, and my job was to stoke the boilers and keep a careful eye on engine pressures. This work continued through to 1941, where we hauled boats on the Berkeley & Sharpness Canal. Later in that same year, I did what a lot of other young men were doing at the time – volunteering for the services – and I went into the army. I started in the Gloucester Regiment, later transferring to the Royal Engineers. After much training, I was involved with the famous D-Day landings on 6 June 1944, where we sailed from the Isle of Wight in American troop carriers.

Fortunately for me, our particular beach landings went without much trouble and we hardly got our feet wet. I then went on to spend the rest of my service life near Le Havre. The following year the war came to an end and, like all other servicemen, the government gave me a free suit to return to civilian life; these were known as demob suits, probably the smartest I have ever been dressed. After that it was back to the familiar currents of the river Severn. At first I worked for the Severner's, and later John Harker's, and both jobs were on the tanker runs from Avonmouth to Stourport, carrying fuel to the dock opposite red rock. These sand stone caves are well known to visitors to Stourport, and this site is the position of the original ferry crossing long before Stourport had its first bridge in the 1770s.

Today, Nellie and I still potter around the Birmingham canals, observing the many changes that have taken place since our boating days. You could say that my boating career took me from the relative tranquillity of the inland waterways, to the excitement and danger of the invasion of Europe.

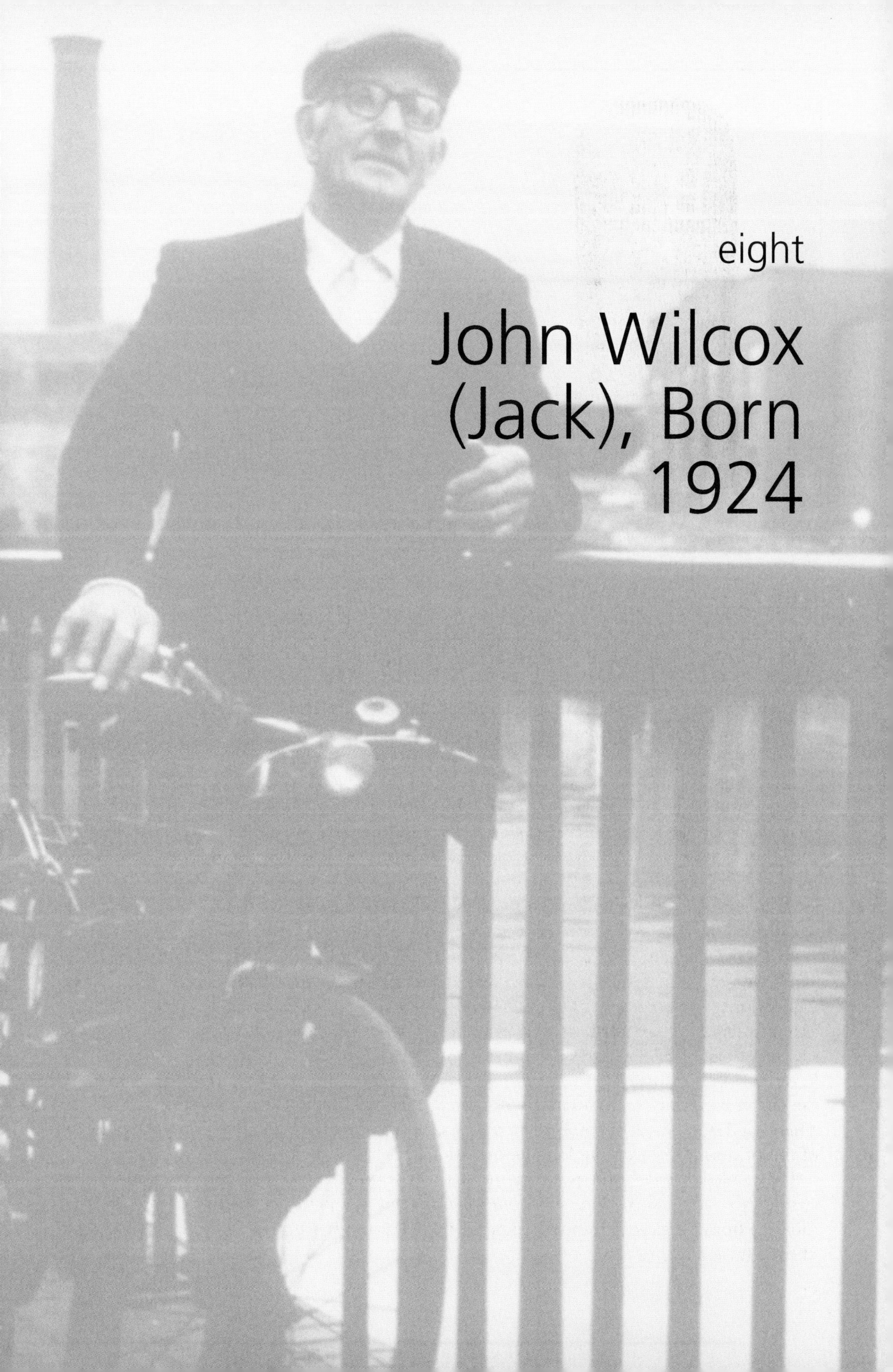

eight

John Wilcox (Jack), Born 1924

Left: Mr John Wilcox, always known as Jack to his friends.

Opposite above: An early pleasure trip in Smethwick. In the background is a fully loaded Elements boat.

Opposite below: T.S. Elements boats on the Netherton branch heading for the tunnel. The tug *Princess Anne* leads, followed by the motor boat *Ben* and two butties. (T.W. King)

John Wilcox

Perhaps it was inevitable that I would follow my father's footsteps into the world of the canals, because as a young lad I often used to accompany him on his boating trips when I was on holiday from school. I can still see him standing there on the counter, steering the boat and staring keenly into the next turn. Meanwhile, I learned to drive the horse and work the locks. This is a lot more complex when you have an animal to control, yet far more interesting. I clearly recall the day when our horse stumbled and fell into the canal; sadly he broke a fetlock – one of the main bones of the foot and we had to get a replacement for him. This is not as easy as it sounds; you just don't unhook one animal and replace it with another – you have to get to know their personality and learn to work with them, it's a partnership.

My father's boss, Ernie Worsey, lived in Whitehall Road, Great Bridge, and even though he was a regular small carrier, he actually hired his boats from a man in Pelsall called Jimmy

Stourport's 'lost basin'. Coal unloading sheds are in the background. This basin is now being restored (2006). (P. Garret)

Stourport's lost warehouses. (P. Garret)

Yates, as did several other small outfits. The three-day boats that Ernie regularly hired out were all of timber construction, with an open hold and a wooden cabin at the rear. The cabins were very Spartan affairs, but each one was at least equipped with a small cast-iron, coal-fired stove, which we kept going in most seasons. In winter it provided that welcome warmth when you had the chance to nip into the cabin, and in the summer it boiled the water for those necessary cups of tea.

Ernie had a carrying contract with a large factory in Great Bridge called Muntz, who manufactured copper tubing. Their coal came from the Brownhills and Cannock collieries, some thirteen miles by water. For some unknown reason to me, my father had a heated argument with his boss, Ernie, over a horse. This resulted in my father and his friend leaving that particular employment and going to work for Elwells, another small Tipton-based canal carrying company. Elwells operated from a yard off Malt House Row, situated on the old Brindley loop that circled Tipton town centre. The gaffer at Elwells was Tommy Brown, and he organised the 'Ampton Boats', as we used to call them, that only worked the Wolverhampton 473ft level.

Some of the Wolverhampton Canal, its branches, and the Wyrley & Essington Canal, were all on the same level, and as a consequence larger than usual boats that could carry up to 50 tons had been designed and built specially for the short-haul transport of coal. However, due to their enlarged dimensions they were unable to go through any of the locks. I remember a Billy Wise working for the firm, and some boat names that included a *Mr Perkins*, *Uncle Jim* and *Ivy*, all fetching and carrying coal from the Cannock Chase collieries. Sometimes they would start out from Beans foundry in Tipton at 10 p.m. on a Sunday night to arrive at the colliery at 4.00 a.m. the next morning. Their boats would line up alongside the floodlit wharf ready for loading, and the coal would arrive in tubs along a railway from the pithead. The tubs were then tipped carefully to distribute the coal in even piles along the hold. At Cannock, the colliery owners had erected crude metal-clad sheds along the towpath to provide a little shelter from snow and rain.

After leaving school at fourteen, I first worked in a factory for a while, but soon had a hankering to work on the canal with my father. At least I had an elementary education, with the advantage of being able to read and write, skills that few boat children had had the opportunity to acquire. Then, during World War Two, at the age of seventeen I went to work for Haywood's, a coal merchant and carriers, based on the Dixon's branch off Horseley Road, next to the Horseley Bridge, Tipton. Two of their boats were the *Banshee* and the *Haughty*, though we used to call the *Banshee* the fly boat because it went so quickly through the water. I partnered with dad, bringing coal to the yard, and also to the Patent Shaft in Wednesbury which had about eight boats per day. We also went over to Saltley to a company called Smith Stone & Knight – I think it was a paper mill. One of our collections was from Hednesford, and while there one day dad had another row, this time over a job with two other boaters named Sam Hickson and Arthur Cope. On occasions there was one journey that paid a little extra to the usual trips because it included a backload of rubbish to Hednesford. This squabble over money, which my father believed he was entitled to, caused a falling out with the boss, and again he moved company.

One of my early jobs was caring for the company's horses and their stables. Horse boats still made up a large part of all boating traffic even in the mid-1940s, and carrying companies usually had their own stables, plus fields where the horses could be turned out when not working, and in some cases their own blacksmiths or farriers. Five horses gave me plenty of work, as anyone who has kept animals will confirm, with daily mucking out and the distribution of feed and water. Horse's tack – that is all of the leather work and buckles that make up bridles and harnesses – needed regular cleaning; don't forget they worked out in all weathers.

My father's name was George, but he was known as Slacky to his mates; he lived in one of the terraced houses in Aston Street, Tipton, this is next to where the Tipton and Toll End Communication Canal used to pass by. After boating for some time I decided to go and work on the bank for a change of pace, but grafting in a factory didn't really suit me so I soon returned to the great outdoors, this time to the small Black Country firm of John M. Wall, who worked three boats from Swan Village, halfway between Tipton and West Bromwich. At Walls, dad and I worked as a team again, working a timber horse boat, and, as before, collecting coal from Brownhills and the Leacroft colliery at Hednesford. This time we were delivering to furnaces on the Ridgacre branch, thus utilising the oldest canal in the Midlands; we also delivered to a firm called Pearson's on the Ryder's Green flight of locks at Great Bridge. Pearson's was a large factory wedged between the canal and Charles Street, and they made different kinds of glass bottles.

At Walls we were given a horse that was completely wild and thus totally unsuitable for the slow plodding and disciplined work of drawing a boat, but we did in time calm it down and get it used to the work. But we were soon on the move again, this time to Elements because it was a better job. T.S. Elements were at that time one of the larger canal carrying companies, far bigger than the one-man arrangements that we were used to. In the past I believe that they controlled a fleet of some 200 craft, but by the time that I joined them, contracts for canal transport were dwindling rapidly due to the great competition from the motor lorry, but I guess that they were still working forty boats or thereabouts. The T.S. stood for Thomas and his brother Samuel Element, who had built up the business from their father George. They also had at least one other brother who ran boats.

Elements had bases in Oldbury and Birmingham, and they used horse-drawn and motor boats; they also ran a handful of lorries. Elements cabins were painted green, with large red panels, and the simple block lettering that spelled out the company name, base of operations and boat name, was in white. At the fore end of the boat was another signwritten decorative panel in red with 'Elements' in white lettering, accompanied with coloured circles, diamonds and crescents to complete the effect. As a company they had long existed as general carriers, but they tended to specialise in building materials such as granite, gravel and sand; other boats were set aside for rubbish removal or coal. I went to work on what was known as the 'Light Run'.

In 1928 a huge coal-fired power station was officially opened by Stanley Baldwin, at the confluence of the rivers Stour and Severn at Stourport, only a few hundred yards from the town and its canal basins. This electricity generating station consumed hundreds of tons of coal each week, the majority of which came down the southern half of the Staffordshire & Worcestershire Canal. This coal was vital to the commercial value of this canal, and the coal came from the pits at Cannock, Rugeley, Hednesford, Baggeridge, and the closer Ashwood colliery, two miles north of Stourton Junction, where the S&W met the Stourbridge Canal. The transport of this coal came to be my life, but I did, on occasions, during winter months when the ice was thick, go and work on the BCN ice-breaking boat at Perry Barr.

However, my journey to Stourport didn't start on the canal, for my boat was some miles from Tipton, and moored near the small rural location called Stewponey, a short walk from Stourton Junction. Ironically, the huge pub that gave its name to this place many years ago, and has been a great landmark for travellers on the S&W and the parallel A449, was demolished in 2001. Some say the early pub's name derived from a corruption of Estapona,

Stourport's Clock Basin and warehouse seen from under Mart Lane Bridge that led into the lost basin. For a long time the bridge was not there, although the Clock Warehouse had been restored, becoming the home of Stourport Yacht Club. The bridge has now been rebuilt (2006). (P. Garret)

an area in Spain where one of its former owners met his wife during the Napoleonic Wars, others that it stems from 'Stew ponds'. As for boatmen, it was a busy but lovely location on the Staffs & Worcs, where I got off the bus and onto my boat. Very early in the morning, me and dad and several other boat captains would catch the bus at Five Ways, Tipton, and travel the eleven miles over to the Stewponey via Dudley and Brierley Hill. If we happened to arrive after heavy rain, our first task was to bucket out all of the water that had collected in the boat. Our horses would have been kept overnight at the Stewponey stables, right next to the toll office and lock. Our boating orders were usually pinned to a notice board affixed to a pole also near the lock. Our cargo was coal slack, a fine, cheap grade of coal, but perfectly good enough for the power station. The journey into and return from Stourport must be along one of the most attractive stretches of canal in the country, as it winds its way through the wooded and sandstone outcrops via Kinver, Cookley and Wolverley. I used to love that slow cruise into Stourport, but I wasn't so keen on sleeping with the bugs that inhabited the bed clothes in the cabin.

Boaters arriving in Stourport these days will go through York Street lock and immediately into the upper basin just as we did. But in the old days there was another basin to the left of this one. It was accessed by going under a small bridge in Mart Lane. After mooring up in this basin, I then left the boat to be unloaded by mechanical grabs while I looked around for an empty boat to bring back to Stewponey. Coal traffic to Stourport by canal came to an end in 1949, when the railway line that had been hindered by World War Two was completed.

Though Elements finished canal carrying some years ago, their lorries can still be spotted, still hauling building materials around the Midlands.

nine

Agnes Radford of Middlewich

Agnes is on the right with her friend Maureen Shaw, at Wardle Lock Cottage, Middlewich, in June 2002.

Agnes Radford was born on 12 September 1943. She now resides in the canal town of Middlewich, just a stone's throw from that intriguing and historic junction of the Trent & Mersey and the Middlewich branch canals. And like so many boating people, the canal with its junctions, bridges and locks always seems to exert some kind of gravitational pull on its past workers right throughout their lives so that they never stray too far from it. On the day that I went to talk to her, Middlewich was preparing for its popular boat show, and boats, traditional and modern, were assembling along the towpath and between the locks. It was a time of nostalgia for old boaters.

The scene opposite has changed dramatically from the carrying era, when salt boats lined the same stretch, loading up and setting off for the Anderton lift or Western Point. While to outward appearances the narrow boats of the Second World War are very similar to their modern counterparts, the boats of today are equipped with every modern contrivance, including central heating, showers and maybe even a computer. In Agnes's day, during cold winter months you stood in the hatches with the doors open to catch some warmth from the coal-fired range. The height of luxury was confined to a few decorative laced plates with coloured ribbons threaded through that her mother had worked with her own hands.

Opposite above: A pair of Fellows Morton & Clayton boats at the Middlewich show in 2002.

Opposite below: Agnes's two sons, Terry and Steven, on the cabin roof of Birmingham & Midland Canal Carriers butty *Ash*. The water cans were not just for decoration – they held the families' water for the day.

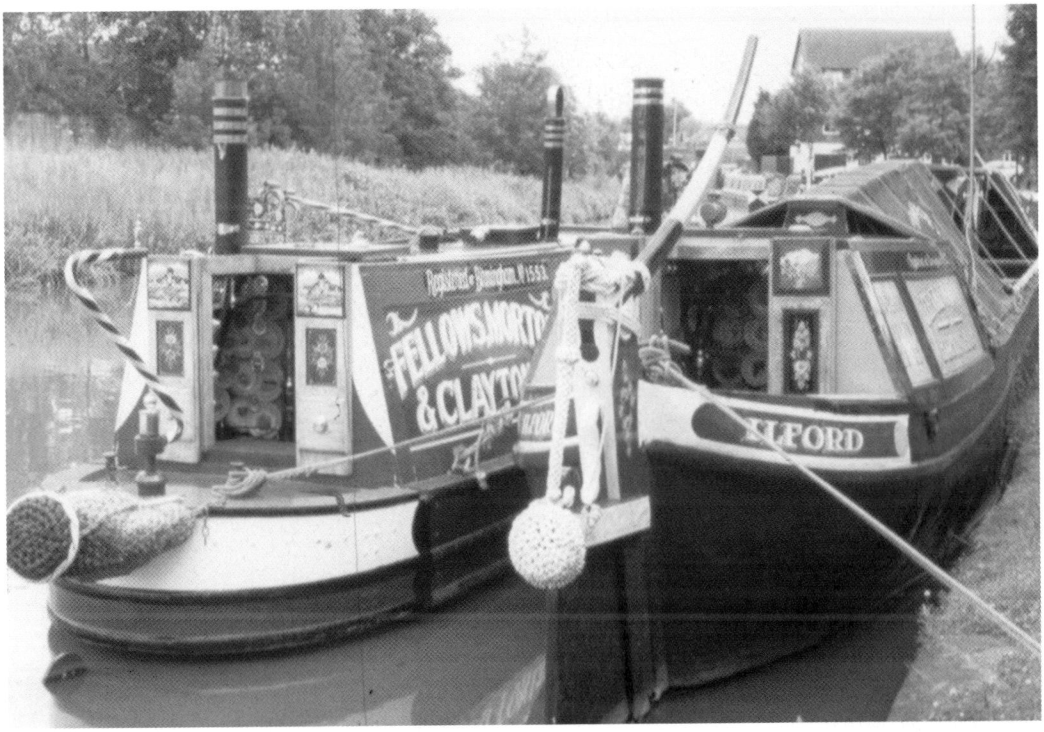
FELLOWS,MORTO
& CLAYTO
LFORD

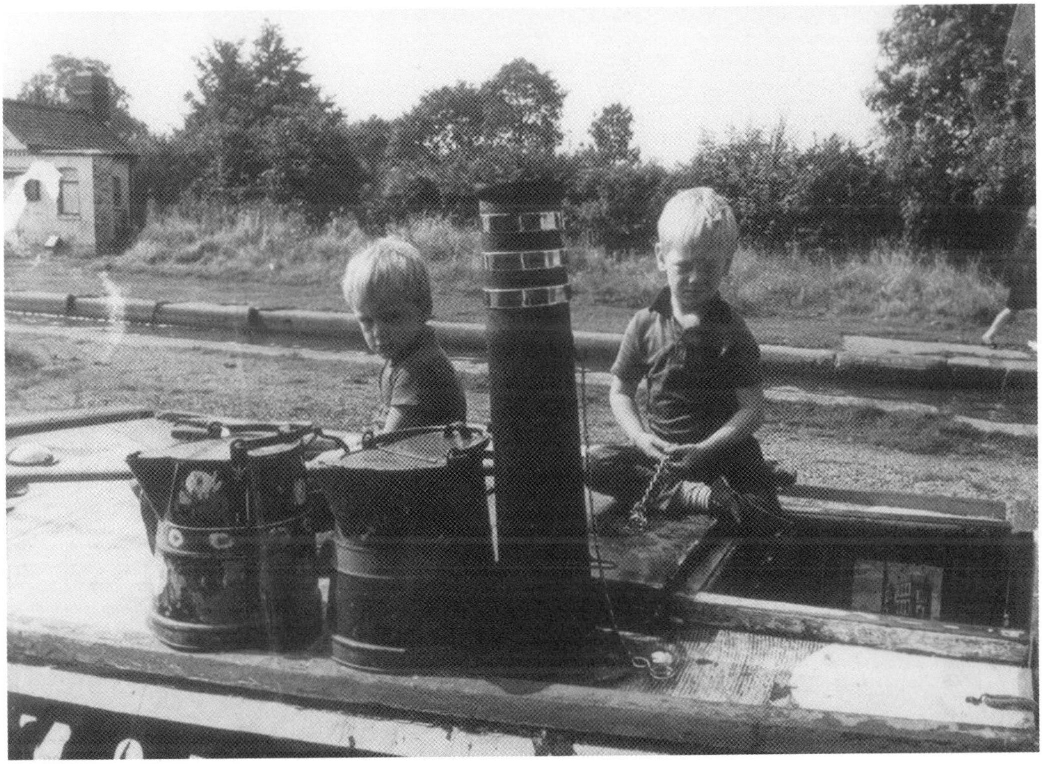

Left: Terry and Steven along with the ever-useful mop.

Below: Mersey Weavers boat *Charles* is left to rot after years of being a home and workplace.

Bottom: Braunston is now used to hosting historic boat rallies. Here we see the distinctive church on the skyline opposite the marina, with Horseley Bridge in the foreground.

Agnes was born in 1943, slap bang in the middle of the Second World War, to Selena and George Radford. This was a time of shifting fortunes and decline for canal carrying. The government had introduced the general rationing of food and other important commodities so that rich and poor were issued with the same books and quotas. In that year, well out of fashion for boatwomen were the voluminous head coverings and blouses from the early part of the century, and in were shorter skirts with less pleats, to save on material. Young ladies who wanted to remain fashionable, and that included those working on the boats, might brown their legs with crème or if that was not available they would use gravy browning, and then get a friend to draw an imitation seam up the back of their legs with an eyebrow pencil. These were tough times for all: canal maintenance was virtually shelved throughout the war, and the vast majority of shipping had transferred to the Atlantic coast because of constant attacks on the Channel shipping by German aircraft.

This is Agnes's account of her father continually changing company to chase the dying trade:

During the last three years of the war, when I was just a youngster, mom and dad worked for Rayners, in the Runcorn and Middlewich area. Much of their work was for the pottery firms at Stoke-on-Trent, transporting china clay and other raw materials from Western Point South along the Trent & Mersey. We had the usual arrangement of a pair of motor boat and butty. Fortunately, I had the motor cabin as a bedroom all to myself. The layout of our cabin was pretty much like others, with a coal-fired range, food cupboard with fold-down table and drawers to stow things away. Cutlery was kept in a drawer under the food cupboard, and toll tickets went into their own little draw by the cabin doors.

Coal was kept under the cabin step, but perishables like milk and cheese went into the stern (or 'starn' as we used to pronounce it) cupboard underneath the tiller to keep cool.

My dad was extremely proud of the appearance of his boat and whenever we approached a town, he would soon have me at work, mopping and scrubbing, polishing the brass, and cleaning all of the rope work, especially the decorative stuff around the ram's head on the butty. Mom was slightly built, but she certainly pulled her weight with the household chores and captaining the butty. When I was about ten, the pottery work in Stoke was fading, so dad took us to work for the Mersey Weavers. It didn't take long to transfer our few possessions from one pair of boats to the next. The Mersey Weaver narrow boats were a late outgrowth of the Mersey & Weaver Ship Canal Carrying Co., transporting a wide variety of goods, but I only remember us loading coal from Manchester and taking it to Runcorn.

Our next employer was Willow Wren, another latecomer to the canal trade, starting in 1952. This new company kicked off with only two pairs of boats, grew to a dozen pairs over the next ten years, and when British Waterways decided to bring their trading days to an end, Willow Wren extended their business activities by taking on about thirty to forty of their boats.

Our pair of boats operated from Western Point, and I can still see in my mind's eye the long line of gabled warehouses, with the distant silhouette of the church and its spire at the other end. The church seemed to be sitting on an island all on its own. We carried mainly copper and spelter, down the 'Shroppie' and into the dirt and grime of the Black Country. As soon as you hit the twenty-one locks at Aldersley Junction, Wolverhampton, the gateway to the BCN, everything seemed to get oily and dirty, and I for one was always glad to be back again at Aldersley, heading toward the freshness and greenery of the countryside. Sometimes we went the other way, using the Anderton lift, and I remember the busy salt trade at Middlewich, when hundreds of tons of salt were tipped down the chutes next to the lift, and into boats waiting below on the river Weaver.

Above left: Agnes's father George in the hatches of a Grand Union boat.

Above right: Selina Radford, Agnes's mother.

Left: George Radford shows his grandson Terry how to use the mop.

Middlewich lock and the old Willow Wren yard behind, 2002.

Our family then left Willow Wren for a short while to try out the blue and yellow boats of the British Waterways fleet. We were now based right down south on the Grand Union Canal at Bulls Bridge, miles away from our former haunts, but you have to go where the work is. We regularly loaded up at Brentford, with paper or timber bound for the Midlands. Much of the maintenance work for the British Waterways boats was undertaken at Bulls Bridge, in the former GUCCCo. docks, and there were dozens of tradesmen employed there.

I can't remember the reason, I suppose it was dad chasing work again, but we returned to Willow Wren. One trip sticks out in my mind: we were taking chocolate crumb from Cadbury's at Bournville back to Braunston when mother became extremely ill. We had to moor up, and she was taken to the nearest hospital in an ambulance. There appeared to be no real alternative for dad, so we continued on our journey south. We were approaching Hatton locks, when a company man came to us on the towpath to inform us that mother had died of influenza. This awful news was of course a great blow to both of us. My workload increased instantly as I had to take mother's place at the tiller of the butty. The company had two boats waiting for us at Hatton so that the cargo could be transhipped. Dad and I made our sad journey back to Birmingham in the empty boats ready for the funeral.

As time went by I met a young man named John Best, who worked for the Grand Union Co. with his parents. Well, after a few outings to the cinema, one thing led to another and I became pregnant. My father, as you can imagine, was extremely angry, but I am glad to say he didn't reject me. I married John at Rickmansworth, and we went to live with his mother

Middlewich top lock, 2002.

and father at Stockers Lock cottage. I had my first two children there before we went back to the boats, this time working for the Birmingham and Midland Canal Carrying Co., and again we had a pair of boats.

Boat people, by the nature of their life and work, have to adapt readily to new bases of operation, and now for us it was the town of Braunston. Braunston was, and still is, a busy three-way junction in Northamptonshire. Here the Oxford Canal travels north for five miles before the remote Napton Junction, while less than two miles east is the entrance to Braunston tunnel. I used to do most of my shopping in Braunston village that lay on a slight ridge just a few hundred yards north of the junction. Some famous and not so famous names of the carrying world have been based at this point, namely Pickfords and Fellows Morton & Clayton for the former, and maybe Willow Wren, Samuel Barlow's and Blue line for the latter.

My greatest difficulty in those days was to bring up three small boys in the confines and attendant hazards of life on a working narrow boat, and we did have our one moment of terror. Terry and Steven were the oldest boys, and they would amuse themselves playing games while being generally sensible to the dangers of the ever-present water, but John was still very small and prone to wander, as little children are, so I used to fasten him by his reins to the cabin side bed. However, one day there was some confusion. I had just unclipped him ready for a nappy change, when boating duties took me out of the cabin. The next thing I heard was Terry shouting that John had fallen in – every mother's nightmare. Fortunately, Terry was quick to act, and had the presence of mind to snatch his little brother out of the canal by leaning over and grabbing his reins. It's that old saying – you can't take your eyes off them for an instant.

Shortly after this episode we left the canal for a while and went to live in a caravan. Our marriage, however, was not working, and I had to leave with my sons in tow. Thankfully, a friend of the family, Mrs Wayne, interceded between father and me – who was still working alone – and we became a team again, but now with three small additions. Dad arranged with the company to take on a butty and we carried on plying the waterways as canal carrying reached its final round-up in the late 1960s.

ten

Bill Tolly

Left: Bill in his garden in 2003.

Opposite: Horse boating for George & Mathews during the 1950s, with Bill's brother Fred at the helm. Staffordshire & Worcestershire Canal.

Bill Tolly of Wolverhampton, born on 25 November 1923

My memory stretches back to the early 1930s, when I was about nine or ten. My mother and father worked for Fellows Morton & Clayton, and had done so for some years. My father was also William, my mother's name was Elizabeth, and our boat was the *Ferret* motor boat, fitted with a Bollinder. FMC had depots all over the country, and I think that we probably visited them all at on time or another, though the one at the top of the Birmingham thirteen was definitely the most frequented. This wharf was situated along the Crescent, but has long gone, and only the remaining short stub know as Cambrian Wharf gives any indication of where the Crescent ran. The loads we carried were extremely varied and included general groceries, copper, spelter, timber, clay, or tubes from Stewarts & Lloyds in Halesowen. As soon as I was big enough, I took over from mother steering the motor, while dad followed in the butty.

We lived on board the boat when on long trips, though we also had a house in Wolverhampton. Mostly we were on the narrow canals, but occasionally we went onto the Manchester Ship Canal alongside ocean-going vessels to load up. It was a bit scary looking up at those giant coasters from the deck of a tiny narrow boat. Sugar in sacks usually went to Broad Street Wolverhampton, so, as you can imagine, we were up and down the Wolverhampton 21 many times. As we ran down the Shroppie toward the Midlands, dad would phone the office at Broad Street. This would be the message for mother to collect a horse from the stables and walk him down to Aldersley to haul the butty up the locks.

We used to refer to the *Ferret* as the Slug, because it didn't swim well, especially along parts of the Shroppie where the pounds were often low in water, though it did fare better where the water was saltier. However, when I was about eighteen we transferred to a much better boat, the *Peacock*. This was the boat we ran throughout the Second World War. The *Peacock* would carry an extra 2 or 3 tons over the *Ferret*.

When on northern trips, we regularly saw boats belonging to the Anderton Co. and Mersey Weavers, and there was a lot of coal traffic on the BCN. Knobstick's cabins – as they were called – were of a lower design than ours, and went much easier through the Harecastle tunnel. In time, dad went on to another boat, the *Rapier* I think it was. I now had the *Peacock* all to myself, though there were many envious grumbles from other boaters because my boat was fitted with the larger Bollinder. Even in those days we were always looking for that extra bit of speed. We were paid for journeys, not for hours. My pay always came through dad, as he was viewed as the captain.

Though FMC had their own mechanic in Birmingham named Jacky Downs, most of the boat operators did their own servicing and repairs, and the things we did to try and hot our engines up! I carried my own set of tools, and regularly tinkered with different jets to try and improve the power. You soon knew when your engine needed a de-coke, too: the power would drop off and it would smoke more. So, as soon as we were moored up for a spell, or waiting to load up, off came the head, and I would use an old knife to scrape away the carbon from the combustion chamber and ports. The company provided gaskets for the engine and soft soap to get your hands clean once the job was finished.

Not all of our trips were north of the Midlands; we occasionally went south to London with timber and copper, though London was a dangerous place to boat during the war when the docks were being regularly bombed. Of course, I had to go and register at the start of the conflict, so I went along to the offices in Horsley Fields. I was interviewed by a nice man, who asked me what branch of the forces I was interested in. When I told him the Royal Air Force he laughed because he imagined that I would obviously enlist for the navy. At any rate, he informed me that as long as I was a good lad, I wouldn't be called up because I was doing a vital job at home.

Fellows Morton & Clayton's Fazeley Street Wharf with Warwick Wharf in the distance, 2001. This was the depot bombed during the Second World War and the area is due to be redeveloped.

One night when Birmingham was bombed, the FMC depot at New Warwick Wharf was hit, and four boats were blown to bits or sunk. The butty *Kildare* was sunk, but has been resurrected to fame with the FMC steamer *President*. Its motor boat *Robin* was carrying tubes, while the pair *Rover* and *Grace* that were carrying cocoa were also severely damaged. Fortunately, the crews had gone to the shelters. Also during the war, I had the occasional spell on the ice boat that was stationed at Sneyd Junction. After the war, I went on to the *Trout*, carrying chocolate crumb from Knighton to Bournville, and sugar in to Knighton. All of the sugar came from Ellesmere Port off the river flats, packed in 2cwt sacks. After the war, dad got a bit fed up with being away from home so often, so we moved to the Wolverhampton coal carrying firm of George & Mathews.

They were situated by the Bilston Street Bridge, and ran around fifteen to twenty boats (I believe their colours were red, with yellow lettering). Now, I was working alongside my brother Fred, and we were in charge of three boats. One was loaded at the Littleton colliery wharf; one was at a Kidderminster carpet factory, while we worked the third, *Florry*. *Florry* was a timber boat with a rear cabin, just enough to provide two beds for the night if necessary, and a stove to make tea. Our beds at this time were made from a calico bag stuffed with straw – sounds crude from a modern perspective, but they were warm and quite comfortable. Of course you had the straw before the horse did. As we moved from one boat to the next, we took the helm, stove and beds with us, and our grey mare, Daisy. Someone else trained her, but she was a pretty good 'oss', certainly better then Elements horses – they never looked as though they were fed enough. George & Mathews had stables at Tettenhall near the Staffordshire & Worcestershire Canal, and we collected our feed from there.

FMC boats at Braunston, 2003. The picture shows the old-style lettering in black and white, and the later style using red panels at the left of the photograph.

FMC's most famous boats, *President* and *Kildare*, at Braunston in July 2003.

Wulfruna Coal Co., Wolverhampton, still selling coal into the millennium.

Then all of a sudden it seemed the coal trade seemed to tail off, George & Mathews like many other coal carriers closed, and I made my last move to Wulfruna, a coal yard on the main line canal at Horseley Fields. The Wulfruna Canal Co. had a full length tug, fitted with an 18HP Russel Rubery, and two- or three-day boats. The coal trips were pretty much the same as for the last firm, with daily runs to Cannock Wood, Hednesford and Brownhills. At eighty I'm still fairly active, looking after the house and garden, especially so since my wife died in September 2002, during the Wolverhampton tremor. And every now and then I pop in to see old friends at Wulfruna, who amazingly are still selling coal at the side of the canal, though these days it's delivered in a lorry.

eleven

Ken and Lilly Wakefield

Above left: Lilly and Ken Wakefield, 2002.

Above right: Ken's sister, Martha Anne, in the hatches of the Potter & Sons boat *Snowflake* with motor *Starlight* in Middlewich's big lock in the 1940s. In the background is Mrs Goodyear's shop where Lilly's mother had her dresses made, and the children bought penny lucky bags. To the right is the silk mill. All these buildings have long gone. The pair of boats have probably just unloaded coal at Seddons. Ken's dad is the figure on the far right.

Cowburn & Cowpar's boat *Shore Lark*.

Ken and Lilly Wakefield talk of their canal carrying days in Cheshire and beyond.

Lilly, born 28 October 1934

My parents, James and Lilly Wain, grandparents and great-grandparents, all worked on the canals; it was no surprise, therefore, that I was born in the cabin of a narrow boat at Longport Wharf, Stoke-on-Trent. At that time mom and dad worked a horse boat for the Mersey Weavers (Mersey & Weaver Ship Canal Carrying Co.) and at Longport the company had their main wharf, warehouse and head office. When tied up at Longport, I remember going into a room called the sail room, where among other things, the side and top cloths for the boats were made and repaired. The room was full of canvas and all kinds of ropes, and a man worked there with a leather apron, sewing with strong needles, setting the eyelets and strings into the cloths. Top and side cloths were normally used to protect the goods from the elements by keeping them dry. Side cloths were permanently fixed to the side of the boat and tied up with strings when not in use, whereas top cloths were taken down and folded away.

In 1936, when I was only two, I almost had a baby brother, but as mother was driving the horse along the towpath one day, the horse spooked and kicked mom hard in the stomach. The next day she miscarried and sadly my brother was lost. Shortly after this family tragedy, mom and dad swapped firms to go boating for Fellows Morton & Clayton, which took them away from the Cheshire locks and south toward London. So instead of destinations at Runcorn or Weston Point, we now frequented places like Brentford or Braunston. For FMC we had the motor boat *Dragon*, powered by a 15hp Bollinder, pulling the butty *Verbena*. Mom's brother Harry helped us to run the two boats; he slept on the motor, while mom, dad and I had the butty cabin. We all got on really well, but Uncle Harry was a terrible tease to me.

After a year or two on the Grand Union Canal, my father longed to return to Cheshire, so when I was about four years of age we all came back to the Mersey Weavers. We were back to horse boating, this time with the *Dart and Aston*. My playground was the area around the Anderton lift, right next to the salt chutes, and we kids used the hand carts for rides. Hundreds of tons of salt came down from Seddon's at Middlewich to be transhipped onto the Weaver Belle that plied the river Weaver. Our narrow boat and many others were constantly up and down the lift, but dad also worked at the company's wharf next to the lift, loading, unloading and bagging materials. Mersey Weavers had stables close to the lift, but we utilised two stables owned by a Mr Walker. Grandad's horse Kip was in one stable, while our horse Jerry was in the other. Jerry was lively to say the least, and only mother seemed to have the knack of catching him if he was turned out into a field. He also had the infuriating habit of rolling over and breaking his gear.

On one occasion, I was in the stable with him sorting out his bedding, when he grabbed me from behind. With my jumper firmly gripped in his teeth, he swung me and dropped me into the manger. He probably thought this a great joke, but from then on I kept well away from him and looked after Kip instead, who was much more appreciative of my care, and had a more kindly nature.

Above: Lilly at four years old on Fellows Morton & Clayton's *Dragon* on the Grand Union Canal.

Left: Ken, aged sixteen, at Middlewich top lock with Potter & Sons *Starlight*. The cabin sides were green with white lettering. The boat is empty and heading for Weston Point for loading, probably with clay.

Above: Children started work young. Here, Lilly sits on a stool to steer *Dragon* with a loaded butty in tow.

Right: Ken's sister, mom and dad on Potters *Sunlight* at the entrance to the Anderton lift, in the late 1940s.

Left: Mersey Weavers horse boat *Longport* on the Bridgwater Canal with Runcorn in the distance, in the 1930s. The boat was actually being towed at the time while Lilly's dad jumped off to take the photograph.

Below: Grandma and Granddad Wain on a pair of narrow boats (the butty is *Ivy*) in one of Dutton locks on the river Weaver.

During the war years we became well acquainted with the American and British servicemen stationed nearby who frequented our local pub that we called the Tip in those days (now the Stanley Arms). A few of them came to visit us on the boats, and they were amazed at how we lived and worked in such tiny cabins (though we did live ashore during weekends, at Harding's Wood near Plants Lock). My very first trip away from the boats was to the British military camp, where we were given a tour of their facilities. From 1939–1945 fruit was extremely scarce, and I remember clearly the first time I ever saw a banana at Weston Point, thinking what a strange thing it was, and when I asked about it my mom of course said that it was for eating.

Captured Italians were also a regular sight as they worked around the lift and its wharves, being identified by a patch on their jackets. As for me, I rarely had another child to play with, so my dog was my constant companion, and we used to go off into the nearest wood together, where I made a playhouse. One day, however, he almost died. He was running about on the top walkway of the lift, when he slipped and fell all the way down. Mother rushed to him, brought him back to the boat and nursed him. He was badly injured, but after a week or so of mom's care, he was soon running along the towpath again, much to my delight. I think by that time dad had had enough of working with horses, so he asked the company to put him on a motor boat, and we transferred to the *Joan*, later the *Weaver*, and lastly the *Walton*, with the butty *Fitton*. We were now hauling gravel from Trentham, just below Stoke-on-Trent, up to Trafford Park in Manchester. After unloading the gravel our boat was thoroughly washed out, ready to be loaded with flour for the return trip.

Ken, born 26 November 1932

I was also born on a horse boat, *Margaret*, but my parents, John and Martha (always known as Patty), worked for the Anderton Co. Unlike Lilly who had no formal schooling, I went to school for five years from the age of nine, but I would rather have been with mom and dad. I was always upset when they went off on their journeys. Fortunately, I was always with them during the school holidays. The boat they used then was the *Portugal*; that later became the *Sunshine*, with *Margaret* serving as the butty. Much of Anderton's work during the 1930s and '40s was for the busy and prosperous pottery works that we referred to as the 'potbanks' that were dotted along and around the canal at Stoke-on-Trent. Finished pottery ware was carefully packed, crated and loaded at Stoke onto the boats for haulage to Runcorn. As a child, I used to go and watch the packers at work, placing the fine straw as a protection between each plate as it went into the crate. Raw materials such as china clay came back to the 'Potbanks'. I also loved to watch Bill Hodgson, the Anderton Co.'s signwriter, at work. Bill was a truly skilful and artistic craftsman, and a nice chap, too, but he would never talk to you while he was concentrating on a job. Anderton's also did the painting for other firms such as Meakin's or Seddon's, but even though Bill painted wonderful roses and castle on their boats, Mr Boddington, the boss of Anderton's, never had him do them for us. Perhaps it was a case of time and cost – I really can't say.

Our journeys up the Trent & Mersey Canal, from Stoke to Runcorn, took in the three tunnels of Saltersford (424 yards), Barnton (72 yards) and the much Longer Harecastle at 2,926 yards. The Cheshire locks, known as heartbreak hill by many boaters, were always hard work, but at least you had a rest at the Harecastle tunnel as the tug pulled you through. I have heard that the Harecastle tug could pull up to twenty boats, but I was used to seeing about half a dozen go through at one time. The tug, equipped with an electric motor, operated much like an electric tram did. An overhead electrified cable went through the tunnel from one end to the other, and the tug, at about 20ft in length, picked up its power via a metal arm extended from the boat. Behind the tug was a ballasted flat-topped boat, while all the other narrow boats were tied behind this. When the tug arrived at the other end, the captain – either Fred, or Sid Mason – turned the tug's pick-up arm around for the return journey. I have read somewhere that captains of boats were supposed to have put out their stoves before going through the tunnel, but I can't say that we ever did.

There were lots of little tricks that horse boaters and motor boaters used to save time and speed things up as they went through the locks, and one of these techniques we called 'strapping in'. Near the hatch we kept a hemp rope that we called a Snubber, and as you went into a lock, the boatman would wind one end of this rope around the gate post, and the other end around one of the dollies at the stern. This would have the effect of pulling the gate closed, and slowing the boat down at the same time, but you had to be nimble footed to get it to work.

From the Anderton Co., we went boating for Cowburn & Cowpars, another northern carrying firm, whose vessels were named after birds, and included the *Starling*, *Swallow*, *Swift*, *Skylark* and *Stork*. These were iron boats, and we had the *Snipe*, with the butty *Lotty*. Cowburn & Cowpars had regular haulage contracts with the big firm of Courtaulds, the boats being fitted out with two large tanks to contain the 20 tons of liquid chemicals that we transported. There was no handballing of items on these runs – the stuff was simply pumped in at one end and pumped out at the other. We loaded up at Trafford Park, and boated down the Trent & Mersey, Middlewich branch, Shropshire Union, and terminated our trip at the Courtaulds factory just outside Wolverhampton on the Staffordshire & Worcestershire Canal near Dunstall race course. A second destination was occasionally to the Courtaulds factory at Coventry, which entailed a trip down the Trent & Mersey, keeping a keen eye on the water levels in the pounds below Fradley. The company's boats with their distinctive maroon cabins were always kept in first-class condition, sporting attractive signwriting, with each boat having chromed metal images of its particular bird on the cabin sides. All of their boats were built at Yarwoods, and fitted with Gardner engines. We then left Cowburn & Cowpars for Potter & Sons of Runcorn, but we could all see that canal carrying was coming to an end as there were less and less boats working the routes. We were now back on the pottery runs, but we also boated coal to Seddon's of Middlewich, the big salt manufacturing firm.

Ken and Lilly have lived in Wheelock, Cheshire for over thirty years, only a few hundred yards from the canal, and though Lilly grew up without the skills of reading and writing, she has taught herself to read, and is making a fine job of documenting the genealogy of her family.

twelve

Joe Safe's Many Years on the Waterways

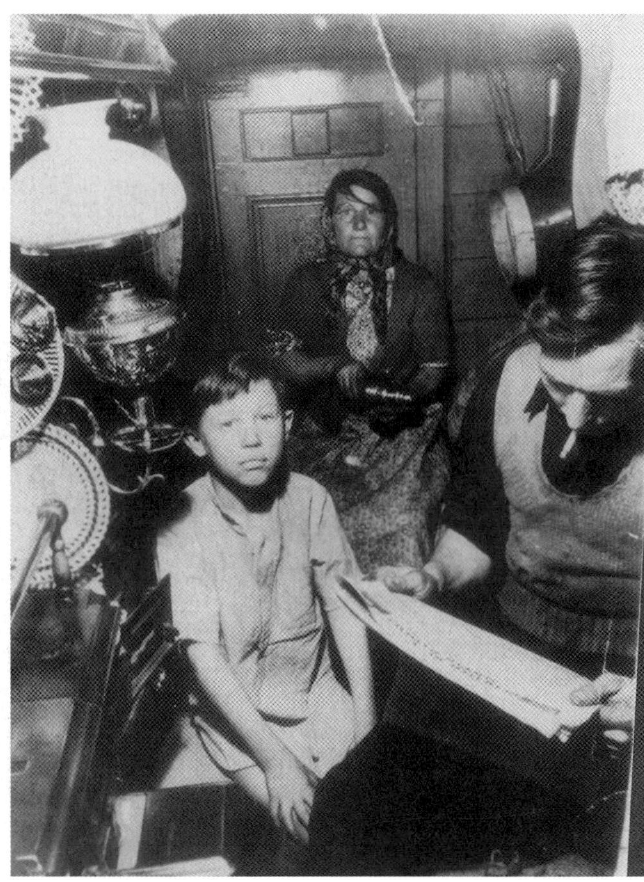

Left: In the cabin of Fellows Morton & Clayton's single motor *Carp* in 1952. Joe is reading the paper with Mary in the background and their adopted son John. They are at Broad Street, Wolverhampton, after travelling down the Shroppie from Weston Point.

Opposite above: British Waterways boats *Dorado* and *Altair* belonged to Charlie Atkins at Croxley, where they are seen unloading coal at Dickinson's Paper Mill. It was whilst working for Clayton's gas boats, bringing diesel from Trafford Park to Langley Green Oil Depot, that Joe vividly recalls being totally iced up for nine weeks some few miles north of Autherley Junction on the Shropshire Union Canal.

Opposite below: British Waterways boats *Elm* and *Ash* at Boxmoor, in the charge of Joe and Mary, *c.*1950. They are taking stone from Stanton Iron Works to West Drayton.

Joe Safe, who reached the grand age of eighty-two in 2004, is an amazing product of the waterways. He has an enthusiasm for life, and a memory that would be called acute for someone half his age. Now well into his retirement, and years after being resident keeper of the electrically operated tidal locks at Brentford, Joe fills in some of his time with the intricate and skilful manufacture of rope fenders. He produces these in the shed at the bottom of the garden of his terraced house in Winson Green, Birmingham.

His working life, however, was spent almost entirely travelling the waterways and visiting innumerable places. The companies he worked for include Willow Wren, Fellows Morton & Clayton, Thomas Clayton, Grand Union Canal Carrying Co., T.S. Elements, several lesser know firms and, at the close of his career, British Waterways. This may give the impression that Joe had difficulties holding down a particular form of employment, but this is certainly not the case; instead it demonstrates the fluidity of work that came with the territory, and most boatmen, and women for that matter, changed canal companies at regular intervals.

Joe was born in 1922, in Wharf Street, Hockley, right next to Hockley Port Loop, to Elizabeth and Benjamin Safe. Benjamin was himself a boatman working for W.H. Bowater, before moving to a Wolverhampton firm called Midland & Coast, before moving again to Thomas Clayton's of Oldbury. One bad winter, his father had to tramp through several miles of snowbound towpaths into Wolverhampton to claim his dole money to feed the family. The rest of the family whiled away the hours playing snakes and ladders and trying to keep warm.

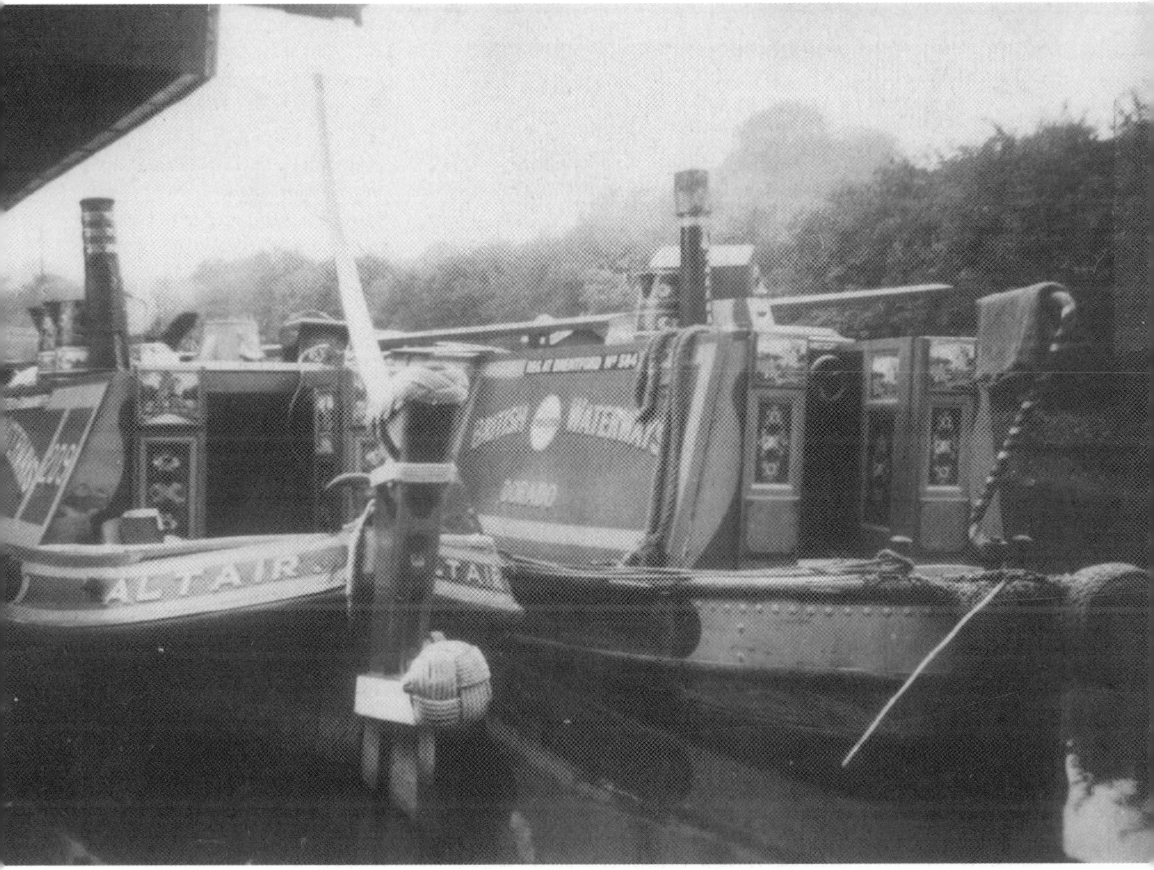
ALTAIR
BRITISH WATERWAYS

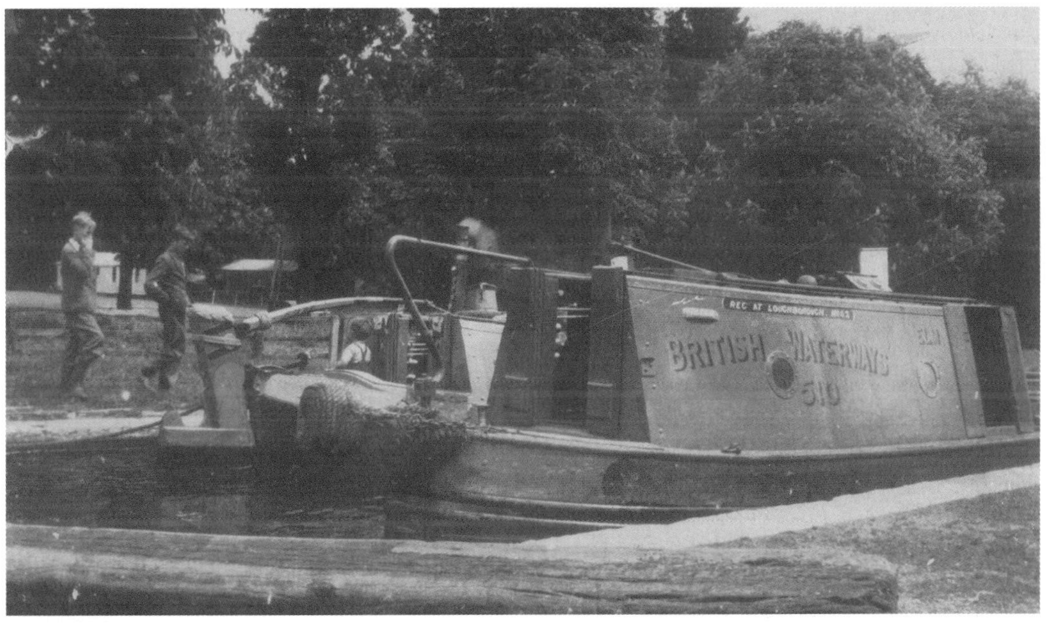

BRITISH WATERWAYS
510

Fellows Morton & Clayton boats passing each other on the Grand Union Canal during the 1940s.

Restored Thomas Clayton gas boat at Ellesmere Port, 2000.

Loaded coal boats at Hednesford Basin.

Worse disasters, though, were never far away whilst working on the canal. The waterways may look beautiful and indeed appear as a kindly and benign environment, but disregard the hazards at your peril. It was when the family were boating for the Grand Union Canal Co. that Joe lost his older brother. This tragedy happened in 1936, when Benjamin was being assisted by his two sons and one daughter, and they had the boats that they called The Hercules *and* Virgins. *It was a frosty New Year's morning and Joe's brother was way out in front preparing the locks for the two following boats. No one knows exactly what happened because there were no witnesses, but one can only guess that he must have slipped on ice at one of the Marsworth locks (Maffers), hit his head and fallen in. Of course, the family then had to go through the awful procedure of dragging their own son/brother from the water. This affair so affected Joe's mom that she spent little time on the canal after this incident, and certainly Benjamin was deeply saddened.*

Many runs for the GUCCCo. with the Mizar *and* Merak *were involved with general cargoes, but included a regular cement haulage run, going from Southam and into Birmingham. Other boatmen on the same routine of around four trips per week included Ike Merchant and his brother Jim, who had a boat each, and Tom Smith. At first the bagged cement – which got everywhere – was taken to a warehouse near Old Turn Junction, and then later to Sampson Road. Every kind of material they carried had its idiosyncrasies, but cement, due to its nature, had to be kept bone dry. This meant in practice that the flooring had to be kept bone dry, which was not always easy. For this, the clothing up had to be thoroughly done to prevent rain spoiling the cement.*

Much of Joe's childhood was spent on the family boat but he did manage to go to school for two years, which, as says in his own words, 'was useful for being good at sums so that I could reckon up the toll charges, and the money we were paid each trip'.

In 1936 Joe left school to join his father, who was now working horse-drawn day boats, collecting coal from the pits around Cannock, and delivering to many destinations around Birmingham and the Black Country. Now they worked for lesser-known canal contractors such as Charles Williams, who had a yard on the Lichfield Road near Aston, and George Rabone who had a yard at Saltley.

At eighteen Joe cut the family strings to mate for various other captains, and boated for T.S. Elements based in Gravelly Hill, Birmingham, and at Oldbury on the old Brindley line, not far from Thomas Claytons. Elements had no live-on-board cabin boats during 1937–1939, and most of their boats were also horse drawn. The majority of their work was coal carrying, and Joe went to work on the

Joe at Braunston in 2003. The photograph was taken by the manager of the marina, Tim Coughlin.

Willow Wren boats unloading timber from Brentford on the Haines branch, Great Bridge, in the late 1960s. (D.W.)

'Light Run' as it was called, which essentially kept the power station at Stourport fuelled with coal from most of the Cannock and Rugeley pits. Boats also collected coal from the Baggeridge Collieries near Sedgeley, which transferred their loads from a short railway to the Ashwood Basin near Stourton. The other busy basin that they used regularly was higher on the Staffordshire & Worcester Canal just below Penkridge at Otherton. The original Otherton basin was 80ft wide and 100ft long, but this short two-boat arm quickly became inadequate and had to be enlarged. Coal was supplied by a short railway that went to two pits, one of which was the Littleton Colliery. The basin was subsequently lengthened to 330ft with a raised pier down the middle so that coal trucks could unload directly into the boats.

There was so much boating activity on the northern section of the busy BCN in those days that there was a kind of tidal flow as the coal boats all headed in one direction, and the men had a sort of ditty that they learned as they went through the lock systems toward Birmingham. It went, 'From the top of the Rushall Canal you come to Mosses two, the Ganzes Seven, the new thirteen and the lousy eleven. With a boat coming up and a boat coming down, and another one standing in the 'ospital pound" (The hospital pound was the stretch between the bottom of the Birmingham thirteen and the Aston locks.)

Towards the end of 1940, Joe decided that if he was ever going to earn any more money, he needed to make a change of company, so he went to the little-known coal firm of S.T. Brant, based on the Soho Loop. Yes, there was more money, but it came with a heavy graft tag attached. Coal from whatever source was usually loaded into the boat from tubs, but it was generally unloaded by hand with a shovel. The unloading rate at Brant's was 5d per ton for Joe and his mate, and they would unload many tons of coal each day to push their wage to between £12 and £15 per week. This was a substantial amount of money during the war year of 1940. In the following year, Joe became attracted to a young woman who was the captain of the well-known FMC boat President, *with its butty* Keswick. *(At that time* President *was fitted out with a diesel engine before being later returned to its original steam power.) Mary Boswell was free to marry because her first husband had died; the problem for Joe was that he only bumped into her on occasions, which was not a good basis for any relationship. His only recourse was to go and work as her mate, which he did the following year. After only two months of working together, they were married at Camp Hill church, Birmingham.*

Mary herself had had an eventful life on the cut, and was a more experienced boat captain than Joe, being seventeen years older. Born in 1905, she was the third of fifteen children to Philip and Anna Ward, who operated the narrow boat Raven *for the Tipton-based firm of William Foster. Many boating couples during these years tended to have large families; however, lots of children on a pair of boats would be the cause of much anxiety, not least due to strict legislation. Boat inspectors were always on the lookout for overcrowded conditions, and the penalties were tough.*

Boat people never seemed to stay with one company for long, and as husband and wife they went on to work for a succession of companies. First they decided to go horse boating for Thomas Claytons, with the narrow boat Forth. *Joe had swapped boats with Charlie Atkins so that he could do the two northern runs each week. Now he was on the Shropshire Union Canal doing regular trips up to Ellesmere Port and Weston Point, and in the process using the Anderton lift. Years later, when they worked for the newly established British Waterways with* Elm *and* Ash, *they actually got stuck halfway down that well-known lift. The main electrical cable for the Anderton lift came across the river, and while work was being done at the ICI factory opposite, the cable was cut. So there they were, suspended between the river and the canal for two hours until repairs had been done.*

During the early 1960s they went 'Willow Wrenning' for about eighteen months with the motor Bittern *and butty* Smew. *This was a company run by Mr Leslie Morton and was based at Brentford. Here they boated coal from the Coventry pits to the Grand Union wharves at Apsley, Nash Mills and Croxley, and timber from Brentford to the Haines branch (Joe says they used to call it the Sheepwash branch) at Great Bridge. But after a falling out with the boss, Joe went for a spell on the land, working for some years on such grand projects as motorway construction before returning to the canals like the inevitable flight of a boomerang. Then in their later years, they found stable employment working for British Waterways at Brentford looking after the tidal locks. Joe and Mary were there until Joe's retirement at sixty-five.*

Opposite: The Anderton lift in the 1960s. (D.W.)

T&S Element's tug and coal boats on the Birmingham Main Line Canal. (D.W.)

thirteen

Roy Nightingale

Roy Nightingale talks about his coal boating days on the BCN:

During the 1930s my grandfather ran a family coal merchants' yard at Pothouse Bridge on the Wednesbury Oak Loop near Bradley. This loop was part of the Old Brindley line that had been effectively cut off when Telford re-routed the line via Coseley tunnel in the 1830s. Grandad Nightingale owned two open boats, but his few workers that include my own father undertook a lot of sub-contracting for the much larger firm of Hickinbottom's who had coal yards in Bradley and Lea Brook, Wednesbury. When he was carrying coal for Hickinbottom's, my father Harold used their boats but his own horses. Subbing out to other firms was a common way of working on the BCN at this time. During the forties, fifties and sixties, much of the coal in the West Midlands came from the Cannock, Norton Canes and Brownhills pits. The Cannock Extension Canal ran from a junction with the Wyrley & Essington Canal at Pelsall Junction due north for a couple of dead-straight miles before turning west toward the Churchbridge locks. A branch left this line to terminate at the Cannock/Hednesford pits. This waterway was probably the most isolated place on the Midlands Canal. From Pelsall Junction northward, there were a succession of pits that included The Grove, Jerome, Fair Lady, Lea Croft and Mid Cannock; I visited them all over the years.

The Cannock pits, Nightingales and Hickinbottom's yards were all on the same Wolverhampton level, so it made sense to utilise the wider 'Hampton' boats, as they were called, because they could carry almost twice the tonnage of a standard narrow boat. Hickinbottom's owned the *Tom* and the *Betty*; they were horse-drawn timber boats having a small cabin at the rear. Inside was a portable stove and two side benches. They weren't designed for comfort but sometimes you had to have a night out in them, and on those occasions you made a crude bed on the side bench using an overcoat to cover yourself.

When Nightingales coal yard closed in the early 1940s, dad split his time steering for Hickinbottom's and cartering, thus his horses pulled both narrow boats and carts. During those school years I regularly had the cane for having dirty hands. This was due to the fact that I had to feed and muck out the horses early in the morning and I was usually too rushed to get my hands washed. While still at school I learned the skills of boating during holidays and days off, so by the time I left school permanently I knew my way around a boat and the local canals. That's how I served my apprenticeship, and it was the same for my older brother Ken.

When I eventually left school, Ken and I worked for my father along with my other brothers Harold and Derek (my youngest brother Neil worked for Toole's in later years). Ken and I had a single horse boat, transporting various coal products to coal merchants, factories and foundries on the BCN. In fact, during all my boating years I never went on another waterway, except for the odd occasion in later years when we took coal over to Stewarts & Lloyds on the Dudley No.2 Canal. We would unload at Hawne Basin after going through Gosty Hill tunnel. Whenever we went through that tunnel I always put the boat into low revs to prevent flooding the towed boat behind. Also, I used to tie the tiller in a central position with two short ropes. This technique was applied on other straight runs when you wanted to nip into the cabin to make a cup of tea or maybe cook something. The first time I went through Gosty Hill tunnel, no one warned me how close the roof came to the cabin and I did a lot of damage to the chimney, crushed the mop and I broke a large water jar. You only make that kind of mistake once!

Above: What remains of the Wednesbury Oak Loop, with Roy reminiscing and pointing out to me where Toole's yard used to be. Just out of sight and round the corner is Pothouse Bridge and what was Nightingales' coal yard, while over on the opposite bank was Toole's. Hickinbottom's was much further along to the left. All have been long replaced by residential housing. (R. Horton)

Left: Legging through Gosty Hill tunnel on the Dudley No.2 Canal. (Dudley Libraries)

Toole's tug, the *Typhoon*, with Ted Griffiths on the tiller, and Len Walton and Arthur Butler on the deck. (G. Walton)

Stewarts & Lloyds coal boats at Hawne Basin. (D.W.)

A rare view of Churchbridge locks in the early 1950s. These connected the Wyrley & Essington to the Staffordshire & Worcestershire Canal. (T. Manning)

One of our regular drops was to the firm of Walton & Browns near Smethwick Junction. Opposite that junction was the entrance to a small loop that we called Tangy's Hole. There was no towpath into this loop, so the horse had to be walked around the roads; whoever was left on the boat would take the long shaft from the boat and pole it through to the back of the boiler house. There, Ken and I would empty some 26 tons of coal by shovel over a retaining wall in less then two hours; today you wouldn't dream of asking someone to move 13 tons of anything by hand. Ken and I got on tremendously well and we would divide our duties; one day he would drive the horse and prepare any locks while I steered, the next day we would change over.

I remember the route we took from the coal fields to Walton & Browns at Tangy's Hole well, because we did it so often. The two-day journey started by collecting boat and horse from Moxley and making our way over to the Cannock collieries via Walsall locks and back to Moxley – one day. Moxley, incidentally, was the site of Thomas's tip and there were always rubbish boats heading that way. The second day took us up the Ryder's Green locks to what we always referred to as Albion turn, but is also known as Pudding Green Junction, and then along the main line to Smethwick. We were paid 1*s* per ton extra for shovelling out.

The Grove on the Cannock Extension Canal. The Wulfruna tug is with the open boat *Audrey*. (W. Tolly)

Our boat was initially gauged after loading at the pit and we were given a ticket to hand in at every toll office on the way, the first being the office at Pelsall Junction where the boat was now gauged by the BCN. There was usually one man at the office up till 9.00 a.m., two men from 9.00 a.m. till 4.00 p.m., and then back to one to cover the end of the day. Gauging took only a couple of minutes as the gauging stick was placed at the regulation four positions along the boat sides. In every toll office was a set of charts, and every boat on the system was on one of those charts. The next gauging took place at Birchills Junction, and the last one took place at Bromford Stop. We also delivered to Guest's Foundry at Hill Top on the Wednesbury Old Canal and Synthite at the top of Ryder's Green locks.

The BCN in those days had their own police who were pretty hot on any misdemeanours by boatmen, and fines were occasionally imposed on the men who flagrantly broke the company's rules. For instance, when we bow-hauled boats going down locks, which was a common practice, it was also common practice to open the top paddles slightly to assist in flushing out the boat. This wasting of water was much frowned upon by a company that jealously guarded its precious water supply, and if the inspectors caught you they would give you a good telling off. As we went down the Ryder's or Factory flights of locks, we used a technique called 'strapping'. As the boat entered the lock, the 'steerer' would drop a short rope that was tied to the stern once around the strapping post on the lock gate. This short post projected above the gate by about a foot and, as you dropped your rope around it, it served the dual purpose of slowing the entrance of the boat and pulling the gate shut at the same time.

Our working day started at about 4 a.m. when one of us had to go and fetch the horse. Dad rented two stables at Bradley and Moxley, and we usually had four or five animals to look after. All shoeing was undertaken by the very skilful blacksmiths at Gospel Oak in between Ocker Hill and Moxley. Once we had a horse named Tommy, who, like many horses, went through a period of lameness. When we arrived at the blacksmiths, he cast his experienced eye over the animal as he walked about the yard. He then commenced making a new set of shoes. In and out of the fire came the red-hot shoe to be hammered and bent over the anvil until it was just right for Tommy. Before the shoes had their final fitting, the blacksmith put a kink at the tail of one side of the shoes. That simple but effective remedy cured Tommy's lameness and he was soon back pulling the boats.

My father Harold had a special way with horses and would regularly take one on that no other person could handle. I remember once we even had a mule on loan for a short period. The firm that owned him were amazed at the way we had him going into the collar. Whenever we acquired a fresh horse, that is to say one that had had no experience of being harnessed and hauling a heavy load, dad would instruct me to take the first week really easy. 'Make a fuss of him', he would say, 'and make sure he is rested and fed well'. This was excellent advice because this careful and thoughtful handling would pay dividends in the long run. I often saw other firms grossly mistreating their animals. This would break their spirit, and often shorten their working life.

After the war we consistently used wooden boats for haulage, many of which hadn't been constructed with the greatest care. Much of the timber had been unseasoned when the boat was constructed. This meant that in operational terms they leaked a lot, and customers were forever reminding us that they were paying for coal and not water. Scoops were kept in the boat and employed daily for bailing purposes. Caulking and tarring were undertaken at intervals but there were always cracks and shakes in the wood that allowed a continual seepage.

One way of countering this problem was to take the boat through what we called a mud hole. Stirring plenty of mud into the water by hitting a mud bank and breaking it up with the prop wash meant that the fine silt was sucked into the fine cracks and temporarily sealed some of them up. On other occasions, chalico – a mixture of horse manure and tar – was applied hot from a bucket which was then plated over with thin metal plate and a handful of nails. Bumping the boat was a sign of poor boatmanship, plus it always produced more leaks, so you did your best to avoid collisions.

A pit mound and stables on the Cannock Extension Canal. The boat is a British Waterways clay boat employed to take puddling clay to bank repairs. In that area there was a permanent gang of bricklayers employed for coping with the continual subsidence next to the waterway. Boatmen called this stretch the Pear Tree Bridges Length.

Coal boats on the Birmingham Main Line in the early twentieth century. The ice boat is on its way past them, while other men are scooping out the ice from the cut and stacking it on the towpath. (Dudley Libraries)

During the winter months we were called on by the BCN to go ice breaking, as was anyone on the cut with a horse. Our meeting point was at the southern end of the Bentley Canal by Forsters Bridge where Jack Evans lived in the BCN lock house. Permanently moored at that junction was an ice breaker. Using anything between six to a dozen horses, we would go crashing through the ice south to Tame Valley Junction and then up the Tame Valley Canal. The Tame Valley was a late canal, having straight sections and twin towpaths. The ice breaker would be pulled by a group on each towpath, each set of horses having one man to drive them. We would go all the way to Perry Bar locks, then turn around and make the return journey. One winter we got stuck with our boats at Pelsall Junction for three days along with Mitchard's and Wulfruna's boats.

During another winter someone had the bright idea of towing the ice boat with a narrow tractor around the intricate bends of the Wyrley & Essington. The tractor ended up rolling down the embankment into a farmer's field and required rescuing.

In the early fifties my brother had to go in the forces for his National Service, so dad joined me on the boats. One day we were returning from the coal fields along the Wyrley & Essington with one of Hickinbottom's boats when John Toole's tug came past. The 'steerer' was Teddy Griffiths, and he shouted over if we would like a tow. 'Besides, it will give your oss a rest', he added. So that's what we did, and I took the horse back to his stable.

While dad was having it easy over to Wolverhampton, Teddy informed him that Toole's were short of 'steerers' and would he like to work for them. That night at 11.00 p.m. we took two boats over to the Cannock collieries in order to meet Toole's tug the next morning at 6.00 a.m. During those years many companies sent their tugs and trains of boats along the Curly Wyrley early in the morning from Horseley Fields Junction, and they included Matty's and Wulfruna's. There were also Leonard Leigh's tugs, the *Christopher James*, *James Loader* and the *Joan* that had contracts to supply Wolverhampton and Birchills power stations. Some of the boatmen were little devils and would do anything to get out in front. When in front they would drop sacks into the locks or in their wake, anything to slow or stop their following competitors.

Leaving the empty boats at the pit to be loaded, I was now steering back the fully loaded Hampton boat *Jeremy* with 'Spottler' Jones following in a second Hampton boat. We arrived back at Toole's yard at around 2.00 p.m. Meanwhile, dad had agreed that we would operate the tug *Typhoon* for them, and I was shown how to start its Lister engine. The 27hp Lister wasn't the easiest engine to get going on a cold day, or any day for that matter. It took two men to turn the starting handle which in turn drove the big flywheel. Once one man had the flywheel turning fast enough, the other had to drop the three decompression levers. Hopefully it would then fire up. Toole's yard was also situated on the Wednesbury Oak Loop – a stretch of water that suffered badly from lack of dredging and weed cutting. It was important to stay on the central track otherwise the prop would soon foul up. There was no weed hatch on the tugs, so if the propeller became fouled, first you tried reversing, then you tried the shaft with the hook, and if all that failed it was strip off and into the canal with a pair of pliers or cutters – even in the winter.

A tug leaving Coseley tunnel, possibly the *Helen* which belonged to Joseph Holloway of Oldbury. (D.W.)

Tug and coal boats on the Cannock Extension Canal. (T. Manning)

Birmingham's Gas Street Basin in the 1960s, before development. (D.W.)

The *Typhoon* usually towed two, or perhaps three, day boats and they were tied in a variety of ways. When empty, two lengths of rope with a short piece of chain in between were slung around the day boat's fore stud, the rope ends being attached to the tugs rear studs. When full, however, the first towed boat was always at the end of the usual tow line some 60 or 70ft behind the tug. Toole's operated as a boat yard and coal merchants; it was managed by John Toole who also arranged road haulage and land drainage. Altogether they probably employed around fifty people, but there were only two people employed in the boat yard and they were Len Walton and Arthur Butler. Toole's had the reputation of building the two biggest Hampton boats, the *Jeremy* and the *Jill*. It wasn't long before I came to loathe steering and operating the *Jeremy* with its bluff bows and massive proportions. It swam like a blunt-ended log, and I tried to break it on several unsuccessful occasions going around turns.

When there was ice on the cut, the *Typhoon* made a reasonable ice breaker, but the jagged ice did a lot of damage to the rivets around the fore end so you had to take it easy.

After that it was my turn to go into the forces, and I entered the Royal Engineers. When I came out I did another spell for Toole's, again working alongside my father, but with all the long hours and poor wages I decided to put my boating days behind me for the comparative comforts of the bank.

Another view of Gas Street Basin before redevelopment.

A rare photograph of the long-gone Tipton & Toll End Communication Canal, as it ran towards Tipton from the grammar school.

fourteen

Alfred Matty's Boats of Coseley

21 August 1970. One of Matty's motor boats towing a day boat into the northern portal of the Netherton Tunnel. This is the *Maureen* looking worse for wear and transporting sludge after dredging operations. The captain is probably Albert Brace who took over the boat from Enoch Clowes in 1969. Interestingly, the old 3,027-yard sign is still on the tunnel entrance, whereas nowadays the distance is, sadly, marked in metres. (D.W.)

With their distinctive Cadmium-yellow cabin boats, Alfred Matty's fleet provided a dash of colour on the BCN, as canal carrying came into its final decades. However, while other large carrying concerns were fading from the scene due to ever dwindling contracts and profits, Matty's actually expanded during the mid-1960s, purchasing boats at rock-bottom prices. Prior to this date the tugs had sported a red livery, but in the 1960s they were all converted to the company's yellow scheme.

In 1964, Alfred Matty and sons left their first small offices at Gate Street, Burnt Tree Tipton, and their canal slipway at Willenhall, for the more substantial canal-side premises at Coseley, where there was a short arm near to Biddings Lane. This arm, situated on the Birmingham to Wolverhampton Main Line, less than half a mile from the northern portal of the Coseley Tunnel – built by Thomas Telford in 1837 – would provide an excellent base for short-haul and maintenance operations on and around the BCN. Deepfields Basin had been in existence for approximately 100 years prior to this time and had been originally a much longer arm known as the Hurst Hill branch, though much of that had been filled in before Matty's took over.

In the early 1900s, the basin and surrounding land had been owned by J.A. Wright, Coal Merchants, who operated their own small fleet of coal boats much like many other coal merchants of the time. Wrights then sub-let parts of their yard to other coal merchants such as Hopkins & Aston, Sid Caswell and W. Dugmore. Each small company busied itself with the transporting and selling of a variety of coal products; stables, horses tack and fodder were all part of the scene.

The *Stratford* heading for West Bromwich through thin ice on the New Main Line. (D.W.)

At that time, Carrons ran a boat-building and repair yard from the basin, and they had facilities for taking boats out of the water in order that repairs to hulls such as caulking and tarring could take place. They were also equipped with large steel drums so that new curved bow timbers could be cut, steamed and bent into place, as many narrow boats were of wood construction.

Before Matty's purchased the basin and surrounding land, the boat-building concern had been taken over by Len Walton, who had started his own business after working for John Tooles boatyard. In the first half of the twentieth century there were many boat repair yards dotted about the BCN, and Tooles yard was not far away at Pothouse Bridge on the Wednesbury Oak Loop. Len and his son Geoff now rented their canal frontage from Matty's and continued to repair working boats before starting to manufacture pleasure craft, an industry that in the 1960s was in its infancy. Walton's Boatyard ceased trading in 1973 when Len retired, and Geoff went to work for Matty's for several years before going on to British Waterways.

From the 1950s through to the 1970s, Alfred Matty's Boats were significant operators on the Midland Waterways, maintaining a total of about fifty boats with around thirty employees. The fleet was made up of a mixture of iron day boats, diesel-powered cabin boats, and at least three tugs, one of which, Silver Annie, *had once been driven by steam. When Matty's took over the yard from J.A. Wright, they also took on their remaining carrying contracts. During these years the company was headed by Frank and John Matty, though the driving force in the 1970s was Susan Roberts and her manager Jim Pearce. Starting years earlier as a secretary for Mr Matty, Susan worked her way up in the company until she eventually became chairman and managing director. Working later with her husband, it appears that she was eminently capable of securing new contracts, which were vital if the company was to succeed in a competitive world where most transport was going to the lorry.*

The *Aldgate* at Dudley Port Junction. (D.W.)

So, what kind of work did Matty's do from the 1950s through to the 1970s? Well, in the first of those decades there was still the remnants of a coal trade, and the tugs were employed pulling short trains of day boats from Cannock Collieries to foundries, factories and coal yards. Then there were the regular dredging and maintenance contracts to keep the waterways viable, plus the disposal of factory rubbish and other industrial waste. Typical of those small contracts was the one the company had with Albright & Wilson's who were a large chemical firm in Oldbury. The Bollinder-powered Maureen and a second towed boat did two runs per day from Oldbury to Dudley Port to dispose of phosphorous waste. Another boat was kept regularly employed taking the waste oil away from the Round Oak Steel Works, much of which had to be ladled from the canal. The Merry Hill Centre has since taken the place of that enormous steel works.

At its peak, the BCN had over 13,000 registered boats; each boat had its number, some of which also received names. Matty's fifty or so boats included the Maureen, Governor, Atlantic, Pacific, Oxford, Greyhound, Silver Annie (Sylvia Anne?) Aldgate and Stratford. The relatively short Governor and Atlantic tugs were ex-ice boats, and those particular examples were two of sixteen built at Bumble Hole, Netherton, Dudley, by William Harris & Sons during the early years of the Second World War. During that period the Governor was used by James Yates of Cannock, hauling coal to Wolverhampton until it was acquired by Matty's in 1950. The Atlantic was 40ft long with ice-breaking bows and was also constructed for Yates. It was sold by BW in 1976 to Matty's, who in turn sold it in 1983. Matty's were often involved in community ventures, such as when they donated a day boat to Dudley Council.

Opposite above: Matty's tug, the *Governor*, in its pre-1960s red livery, towing two boats of day trippers, *c.*1952. Trips were popular in the 1940s and 1950s for employees, friends and relatives. Steering the *Governor* is Jimmy Wildey with Sylvia Matty, while sitting at the front is Susan Roberts, with Mr Harrison in the middle waving. The boy at the fore end is probably Eric Matty, with Neville Roberts standing on the gunwale. (Dudley Archives)

Opposite below: The Old Main Line near Oldbury, *c.*1968. Enoch Clowes is on the *Maureen*, towing a second boat; both are transporting phosphorous waste to Dudley Port. (D.W.)

This particular boat, built in 1943, was renovated by the Manpower Services Commission to give youngsters the opportunity to experience a day on the canals. Named Matty Butty *it was re-launched by the mayor of Dudley David Gaunt at Hawne Basin in 1981.*

After 1980, even Matty's could no longer sustain a canal transport firm and they sold the basin and land to the crane hire firm of Dewsbury & Proud, who were still operating from that base in 2004. The Governor *lay on the banks for some years until 1986 when it was restored.*

Matty's boatyard at Coseley, looking south towards Tipton with Biddings Lane Bridge in the distance, *c.*1970. The firm's offices were in the white building at the rear on the left, and Walton's boatyard occupied the canal frontage immediately in front of those offices. (Dudley Archives)

Birmingham Main Line Canal, Deepfields Arm, May 2004. (R. Davies)

A restored *Governor* at Longwood Junction, now belonging to Mr John Humble, and in 1940s livery, 2004.

Walton's boatyard with Frank Matty on the left, then Len Walton and Geoff Walton, 1964. (G. Walton)

The tug *Pacific* on the Bradley arm, steered by Albert Brace, 1983. (G. Walton)

Maureen cutting through ice on the main line, *c.*1965. (D. W.)

fifteen

The Work of the Ice Breakers

It is generally recognised that it was the efficiency of the growing railway system that drove the nails into the coffin of the canal trade, but there were other important factors, one of which was the wintry scourge of ice and snow. When freezing winds blew and temperatures plummeted, the surface of the canal quickly turned to ice. If the depth of that ice went over 3 or 4in, then whole fleets would become unmovable – and so would their valuable cargoes.

We are used to seeing very mild winters during recent years, but working boatmen and women remember some very harsh conditions during the 1940s and 1960s. In the late 1940s at Napton, many boats were frozen into the bank belonging to Thomas Clayton's, Samuel Barlow's and the 'Ovalteeners'. The ice boats were unable to get through to this remote rural location and the families were forced to stay put for several weeks. Fortunately, they were the sharing types, and those that had coal shared it with those without, and those with drinking materials also shared their cargo; local farms supplied stuff like bread, eggs and bacon. When dozens of boats were frozen to the bank in this way for indeterminate periods, carrying companies started to lose their contracts to rail and road, especially to road transport after the First World War.

To try and keep the channels open, canal companies operated their 'Ice Boats' right up to the 1950s, probably one of the most hazardous jobs on the waterway. The design and operation of these craft varied slightly from region to region, but in essence they operated on very similar principles. Generally, they were horse drawn, though there were some engine-driven types. They were usually half the length of other boats, and their thick, rounded timber hulls with pointed prows were, in most cases, covered with overlapping iron sheets for protection. For many months the ice boats had been beached near a maintenance depot, some even being partly sunk to preserve the timbers; but at the first sign of a freeze, the water was pumped out, men pressed into service, and a team of horses assembled. Often railway horses were employed as motive power to make up a pulling team of anything from four to a dozen, or even fifteen, animals. The ice boats would occasionally start during the hours of darkness, which would make an already difficult job even more hazardous.

The horses would usually be attached to the boat at the mast, and led by one or two drivers jogging along beside them. A team of six to ten men dressed in thick overcoats would board the boat and arrange themselves in two lines down the centre of a slatted deck, and hang on to a centre rope attached to two or more short masts. As the boat crashed into and onto the quickly forming ice at around 5 to 8mph – a fast trot or even a canter – the men would rock the boat from side to side and hopefully break up the ice into pieces. Coat tails often went into the icy water as it washed over the gunwales. On the Cheshire canals, a pony was sometimes tethered to the rear of the boat to assist the 'steerer' around the tighter bends. The pony would also be useful as a reverse gear if the boat ever got stuck on, or even under, the ice. This ice-breaking task was dangerous for both men and horses, and it was not unknown for either to slip and fall in. The loud cracking of the ice, sometimes heard for miles, heralded the coming of the ice boat, and then the crack of the whips could be heard as the leading horses rounded the bend in a cloud of steam.

In preparation for winter conditions, the company's boat passed through with a load of ash or sand, leaving a pile at each lock. Then, when needed, the lock keepers would scatter a layer over the lock approaches and sides, under bridges and balance beams, then set to work chipping ice and snow from the lock gates. Of course, all of this only broke the ice, it did not get rid of it; and when there were plenty of hands to be had – and many of the boaters would have joined in the grand clearing effort – the ice was scooped off the surface, or even floated from lock to lock as on the Trent & Mersey. Meanwhile, the boaters would be waiting for the canal to be cleared. Then there would be a dash to get going as soon as the ice boat had passed.

Thomas Clayton oil boat struggles through ice on the Old Main Line near Oldbury in the mid-1950s. (W. King)

Coal boats on the Wyrley & Essington Canal, coming from the collieries at the end of the Cannock Extension Canal, *c.*1955.

A beached ice breaker on the Llangollen Canal near the Ellesmere maintenance yard, mid-1950s.

Snow finally clearing from the Stourbridge locks with Dadford's shed and glass cone in the distance.

Lapworth Junction in the snow, 2004.

Thomas Clayton boat cutting through ice sheets on the Wednesbury Old Canal, *c.*1965. (D.W.)

Other titles published by The History Press

The Birmingham Canal Navigations

RAY SHILL

The BCN network developed over one hundred years and served the busiest industrial region of the country – earning Birmingham the nickname of 'Little Venice'. Ray Shill examines the industrial archaeology of the network in *The Birmingham Canal Navigations.*

07524 2767 9

Boats, Smoke, Steam and Folk

ROBERT DAVIES

Exploring the canals of the Midlands, this book, with maps and detailed walks, will encourage the reader to move from his armchair and into this living piece of history. Included are interviews and memories of those who worked the canals, albeit in the twilight years of the fifties and sixties when road transport was taking over the role of moving bulky loads around the country.

07524 1765 7

The Inland Waterways Association

DAVID BLAGROVE

Sixty years ago, a small band of enthusiasts gathered together to form The Inland Waterways Association. From those early beginnings, The Inland Waterways Association grew into a group of 17,000 members. Illustrated with many captivating photographs from the 1940s to the present day, this provides an informative record of IWA's fight to restore Britain's waterways.

07524 3158 7

The Grand Union Canal (North) Towpath Guide

NICK CORBLE

Working its way from Salford Junction outside Birmingham to Milton Keynes, this illustrated guide covers the northern part of the Grand Union Canal, accompanying the guide to the southern half published in 2005. *The Grand Union Canal (North)* is the third in a series of Towpath Guides from Tempus.

07524 3083 4

If you are interested in purchasing other books published by The History Press, or in case you have difficulty finding any of our books in your local bookshop, you can also place orders directly through our website

www.thehistorypress.co.uk